Larger -thAN- Life Activities

By Susan L. Lingo

STANDARD PUBLISHING

Cincinnati, Ohio

DEDICATION

*May the favor of the Lord our God rest upon us; establish the work
of our hands—yes, establish the work of our hands. Psalm 90:17*

Worship the Lord with gladness; come before him with joyful songs. Psalm 100:2

Larger-Than-Life Activities

Copyright © 1998 Susan L. Lingo

Produced by Susan L. Lingo
Cover design by Liz Howe
Illustrated by Marilyn G. Barr

All Scripture quotations, unless otherwise indicated, are taken from the HOLY BIBLE,
NEW INTERNATIONAL VERSION®. NIV®. Copyright © 1973, 1978, 1984 by International Bible Society.
Used by permission of Zondervan Publishing House. All rights reserved.

Scriptures marked ICB quoted from the International Children's Bible, New Century Version,
copyright © 1986, 1988 by Word Publishing, Dallas, Texas 75039. Used by permission.

Published by The Standard Publishing Company, 8121 Hamilton Avenue, Cincinnati, Ohio 45231.
A division of Standex International Corporation. All rights reserved. Printed in the United States of America.

05 04 03 02 01 00 99 98   5 4 3 2 1

ISBN 0-7847-0782-0

CONTENTS

HUMONGOUS HUMANS & CREATIVE CHARACTERS

COLOSSAL CLASSROOMS & DYNAMITE DISPLAYS

MAMMOTH MUNCHIES

MOST CRAFTS ARE SELFISH!

What? Crafts can be selfish? Isn't that going a little overboard? Well, maybe just a bit. But let's face it…most children's craft projects are self-expressions of self-created ideas made by one to be enjoyed by one. So what's the answer? Simple! Make crafts that are *cooperative* and *service-oriented!* Cooperative service crafts are made by many to be enjoyed—and used—by many. Not forgotten on refrigerator doors or dusty shelves, the service crafts in *Larger-Than-Life Activities* are made to be happily used and enjoyed by the lucky recipients of your kids' creative talent.

HOW DO COOPERATIVE SERVICE CRAFTS WORK?

As easy as 1, 2, 3!

1. Understand the need. In each craft activity, children learn *why* they're making the craft and *who* they're serving. Scripture, biblical concepts, and Bible stories form the basis of each craft and provide children with a solid understanding of others' needs and how to meet those needs in creative ways.

2. Create 'n' cooperate. Through small groups, large groups, pairs, and trios, children work interactively to construct every craft project. Kids build self-esteem, great communication skills, and a sense of community. Self-worth through team effort—isn't it amazing?

3. Give 'em away! Each craft idea in *Larger-Than-Life Activities* is really a service project meant to be given away to the church, another class, or the community. What a feel-good concept for everyone!

Creativity, cooperation, a sense of community and giving—what could be more fun? GIANT crafts! **Huge** crafts! **Gigantic, colossal, humongous** crafts! Every service craft idea in *Larger-Than-Life Activities* is larger-than-life and fun to make. Older kids hard to motivate? Not any more! No sissy paper doilies, no cut-n-paste clones, no paper plate boredom. These are big projects with big appeal—guaranteed!

So what are you waiting for? Gather your kids, stir your imagination, and dive into *Larger-Than-Life Activities* for big fun—and GIANT giving!

Chapter 1

SUPER SCULPTURES

Humongous houses, colossal cars, touch-the-sky towers, an amazing ark—and much more!

PVC for You and Me!

So let us try to do what makes peace and helps one another. Romans 14:19 (ICB)

Bible Craft Concept
We can build love through peace, victory, and caring in Christ.

Crafty Components
You'll need a Bible, colored vinyl electrical tape, duct tape, scissors, hinge clothespins, picture-hanging wire, ribbon, clear tape, permanent markers or crayons, and scraps of PVC pipe.

GET READY...

Set out the PVC pipe, colored electrical tape, ribbon, scissors, clear tape, picture-hanging wire, clothespins, duct tape, markers or crayons, and scissors.

GET SET...

Gather children around the craft materials. Ask:

▶ **When is a time you did something to build love or friendship with someone? How did you feel?**

▶ **Why is it important to build love and friendship with others? How does it help our own hearts? others' hearts?**

▶ **What are ways to build love? to build friendships? to build caring?**

Say: **It's not always easy to build love with others, but it is always important. Let's see what the Bible tells us about loving others—or at least trying to!** Ask a volunteer to read aloud Romans 14:19. Then say: **Jesus wants us to build love with others by serving them, by caring for them, by helping them, and by doing kind things for them. When we build up love in others, we spread Jesus' love and promote**

Christ's peace, victory, and caring. Peace, victory, caring—those are real love-builders!

Hold up a piece of PVC pipe and say: **This is called PVC pipe. We can remember those letters through these words: Peace, Victory, and Caring—just what Jesus wants us to do to spread his love to others. Let's use PVC pipe to build a little love. We'll work together to build a beautiful sculpture on which younger kids can hang their artwork.**

GET CRAFTIN'...

Have kids form two groups, the Architects and the Artists. The Architects can use duct tape and electrical tape to connect the PVC pipe into a crazy frame, as tall and wide as you have pipe to construct. The Artists can wrap clear tape and ribbon around the pipe, then use permanent markers or crayons to add decorative squiggles and wiggles to the tape and PVC pipe. When the sculpture is complete, let each child cut a 10" length of picture-hanging wire and use it to attach a hinge-style clothespin to a section of pipe. Be sure there are several inches between each clothespin so artwork and other papers can be displayed without overlapping. As you work, talk about ways you can build love and friendship with others during the coming week.

After the sculpture is completely finished, let children admire their cooperative efforts and affirm their creative work. Then invite children to carry their Peace, Victory, Caring sculpture to a classroom of younger children and present their masterpiece. Have your children explain to the younger class that the PVC sculpture can be used to display their artwork. Then demonstrate how to clip a paper to a clothespin. End by asking several older children to explain what the letters "PVC" stand for and why it's important for us to build love and friendship with others.

Crafty Tips
▶ If you're short on PVC scraps, you can purchase this plastic pipe from any hardware or building supplies store. Use a coping saw to cut the pipe into desired lengths before class.

Crafty Tips
▶ Suggest that younger children draw colorful pictures of how they can spread Jesus' love to others. Have kids draw pictures on white construction paper, then hang the pictures on the PVC sculpture. Display the sculpture and artwork in the entrance to the church or sanctuary to spread colorful joy to everyone!

Come to the Cross

Come to me, all of you who are tired and have heavy loads. Matthew 11:28 (ICB)

Bible Craft Concept
We can leave our troubles with Jesus.

Crafty Components
You'll need a Bible, duct tape, newspapers, gold braid or rickrack, markers, construction paper, tacky craft glue, a medium-sized box, several paper grocery sacks, one 2'-by-½" dowel rod, and one 4'-by-½" dowel rod.

GET READY...

Place craft materials on the floor. Set the box, newspapers, glue, gold braid or rickrack, and construction paper together. Place the dowel rods, grocery sacks, and duct tape together in another area.

Check with the church leader to find a good time for children to present their colossal craft to the entire congregation. Ask for slips of paper and pencils to be handy for church members.

GET SET...

Gather children and ask:

▶ **What is something you've said or done wrong?**

▶ **How did you feel knowing you had said or done this?**

▶ **Can we do anything to take back the wrong words we say or the hurtful things we do? Explain.**

Say: **We've all said and done things that God tells us are wrong. That's what sin is. In fact, the Bible tells us that everyone has sinned.** Ask a volunteer to read aloud Romans 3:23. Then say: **It feels pretty awful when we say and do wrong things—like we're carrying a heavy load inside our hearts. So how do we lighten the load? How do we make things right and become God's friends?** Encourage children to share their thoughts. Then have another volunteer read aloud Matthew 11:28. Ask:

▶ **What does Jesus' forgiveness do for us?**

Say: **When we bring our heavy troubles to Jesus, he takes them away and lightens our loads. Jesus wants us to give our heavy loads to him so he can take them away through his forgiveness. When we bring our troubles, our hurts, and our sins to the cross of Jesus, we become God's friends. And that feels wonderful! Let's make a really neat BIG cross to remind people in our church that we can bring our heavy troubles to Jesus' cross.**

GET CRAFTIN'...

Form two groups, the Box-Basers and the Cross-Crafters. Have the Box-Basers stuff newspapers snugly into the empty box to make the box sturdy. Then instruct them to tape the top of the box closed and to carefully use scissors to punch a small hole in the center of the widest end of the box. Then have the Box-Basers use tacky glue, construction paper, and gold braid or rickrack to decorate the base. Write the words "Come to the Cross" on the front of the box.

Have the Cross-Crafters make a cross from the dowel rods. Use duct tape to tape the shorter dowel rod across the upper third of the longer dowel rod. Crisscross the tape to hold the "crossbeam" securely in place. Then show the children how to gently crumple and twist the paper grocery sacks into long pieces of "wood." Tape the pretend wood to the dowel rods to make them appear treelike. Show children how to hide the duct tape behind the cross or how to roll pieces of tape to hold the paper sacks in place.

When the base and cross are finished, slide the bottom 6" of the cross into the hole in the box. Secure the cross to the base using duct tape. Cover the tape with green paper "grass" or paper "flowers."

When children are ready to present their gift to the congregation, have them cooperatively carry in the cross. Explain to the church members why the children made this beautiful cross to share, then ask two children to read aloud Romans 3:23 and Matthew 11:28. Encourage members of the congregation to write one problem or worry they'd like to leave at the cross on a slip of paper. Then ask people to come forward and slide the slips of paper into the twists and folds of the cross. End by having children lead the congregation in singing "Jesus Loves Me."

Crafty Tips

▶ Trade the cross from classroom to classroom throughout the year. Have each class compose encouraging messages for the class who will receive the cross next week and slide the messages in the twists of "wood."

Crafty Tips

▶ Keep the cross in the entry to your church building. Let classes take turns decorating the cross according to seasons and holidays. For example, make ornaments to hang on the cross at Christmas, decorate the cross with hearts and Scripture verses on love for Valentine's Day, and decorate the cross with flowers in spring.

Awesome Ark

Obey the Lord your God. Deuteronomy 27:10

Bible Craft Concept
We can obey God.

Crafty Components
You'll need a Bible, a saw, construction paper, a Hula Hoop, paper grocery sacks, duct tape, scissors, paper plates, cotton balls, fishing line, glue sticks, and twelve 4'-by-½" dowel rods.

GET READY...

(Saw the Hula Hoop in half before you begin.) Place the dowel rods, duct tape, and paper grocery sacks in one area of the room. Set the construction paper, scissors, and one glue stick in another area. Place the paper plates, glue sticks, and cotton balls in yet another part of the room.

GET SET...

Have children sit in a group and ask:

▶ **What does it mean to obey your parents? your teacher? God?**

▶ **What happens when you don't obey?**

▶ **Why is it important to obey God?**

Say: **Remember the story of Noah and the ark? Noah found out how important it is to obey God. What might have happened if Noah hadn't obeyed?** Encourage children to tell their ideas. Then say: **The Bible tells us a lot about obeying God. Let's read what the Bible says.** Ask several volunteers to read aloud Deuteronomy 27:10; Deuteronomy 6:2; and Acts 5:29. Then ask:

▶ **How can we obey God?**

▶ **In what ways can we encourage others to obey God?**

Say: **When we remember the story of Noah and the ark, we also remember the importance of obeying God. Let's help younger kids learn more about Noah and how he obeyed God. We can build a big ark to remind them that obeying God is the best thing we can do!**

Crafty Tips
▶ Instead of a Hula Hoop rainbow, simply use a stiff paper arch.
▶ Place an old blue bedsheet around the ark to create "waves."

GET CRAFTIN'...

Form three groups: the Ark-itects, the Cloud-Creators, and the Animal-Arrangers. Have the Ark-itects work together to construct an ark "shell" by using duct tape to attach dowel rods according to the illustration. Use four dowels for the base, four dowels for the corner supports, and four dowels for the top of the ark. Crisscross the duct tape to tightly secure the dowel rods. (See diagram below.) Securely tape the Hula Hoop half to the back corners of the ark shell to make a "rainbow." When the ark shell is complete, have the Ark-itects tape wide strips of grocery sack to three outside walls of the ark. For a more realistic touch, show children how to use black markers to draw "grain" in the paper "wood."

Have the Cloud-Creators tape tinsel to the lower half of several paper plates, then glue cotton balls over the tinsel to make pretend rain clouds. Cut 10" lengths of fishing line and tape one cloud to the end of each piece of fishing line. Then tape or tie the other ends of the fishing line to the Hula Hoop rainbow. When the clouds are suspended, have the Cloud-Creators help the Animal-Arrangers or Ark-itects.

Animal-Arrangers can create several large construction paper animals such as elephants, giraffes, horses, or bears. Let children's imaginations go wild and encourage them to use extra cotton balls for bunny tails and fringed paper for spiky manes or flowing tails. When the animals are done, glue them to the inside walls of the ark.

After the entire ark is complete, invite children to sit around the ark as you read them the story of Noah and how he obeyed God. Then have children donate their special creation to a classroom of preschoolers. If you have older children, they may wish to act out the story of Noah and the ark as they invite the preschoolers to help by making appropriate animal noises. Encourage the preschoolers to carefully crawl aboard the ark and care for it as Noah cared for the real ark.

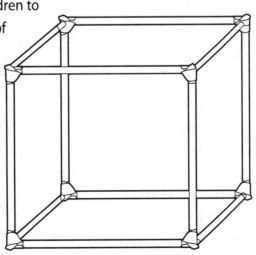

Creation Celebration

God has planned a time for every thing and every action... Ecclesiastes 3:17 (ICB)

Bible Craft Concept
God is in control of everything.

Crafty Components
You'll need a Bible, construction paper, gift wrap, glue, markers, clear packing tape, scissors, and white paper. You'll also need seven various-sized boxes for stacking one on top of the other. Be sure the total height of the boxes is at least 3'.

GET READY...

Place the boxes around the room and the remainder of the craft materials in the center of the room. Photocopy the "Days of Creation" rhyme from this activity.

GET SET...

Gather children in a group. Ask several volunteers to recite the alphabet or to count to ten. Then ask:

▶ **Why did you say the numbers or letters in the same order each time?**

▶ **What are other things that have a correct order?**

Encourage children to name days of the week, months of the year, hours in a day, their phone numbers, and their addresses. Then say: **When God created the world, he created it in a specific order. Do you remember that order? Let's do a finger rhyme to review the order in which God created the world.**

DAYS OF CREATION

Day one, let there be light—
Day two, the air so bright.
Day three, trees and plants—
Day four, the sky-lights dance!
Day five, birds and fish we find—
Day six, animals and humankind.
Day seven, God's day of rest—
And this is how the world was blessed!

Hold up a finger for each day of creation.

Say: **God put everything in its right place and order. That's because God is in control of the whole world. The Bible tells us that everything God has done has its own time and place.** Ask a volunteer to read aloud Ecclesiastes 3:1-15 and 17. Then ask:

▶ **What is God in control of?**

▶ **Why is it good that God is in control instead of us?**

Say: **When we know the order that God created the world, we realize God's control. We know that God's control is perfect and perfectly in order. Let's help another class learn the order of God's creation. We'll make a giant tower to remind everyone that God's order is perfect.**

GET CRAFTIN'...

Form seven small groups and give each group a box. Assign each group a number from one through seven according to descending box size. Box one should be the largest; box seven the smallest.

Tape the flaps of the boxes closed. Then invite children to cover their boxes with construction paper or gift wrap. Have each group cut out a giant numeral that corresponds to its number. Glue the numeral to the widest side of each box. Then have children create illustrations that correspond to each day of creation. For example, the group with day four might create a construction paper moon, sun, and stars. Or the group with day seven might illustrate animals and the two people sleeping to symbolize rest. Consider embellishing the boxes with tactile items such as cotton balls, sandpaper, silk flowers, feathers, and shiny foil stars.

When the boxes are finished, review the "Days of Creation" rhyme as you stack the boxes in their correct order. Then tumble the boxes and repeat the activity. When your children are through playing with their craft project, have them donate the stacking tower to a preschool classroom along with a photocopy of the "Days of Creation" rhyme. Encourage your children to read the creation rhyme to the younger children as they help the preschoolers stack the boxes in the correct order.

Crafty Tips
▶ Use this colorful giant tower to help tell the story of the Tower of Babel or of the walls of Jericho.

Crafty Tips
▶ Stuff the boxes with newspaper to make them sturdier.

Tremendous Trellises of Joy

You are filled with a joy that cannot be explained. 1 Peter 1:8 (ICB)

Bible Craft Concept
We can share our joy in Jesus.

Crafty Components
You'll need a Bible, colored construction paper, white paper, a stapler, glue sticks, precut bulletin board letters, clear packing tape, string, and two tall wooden trellises.

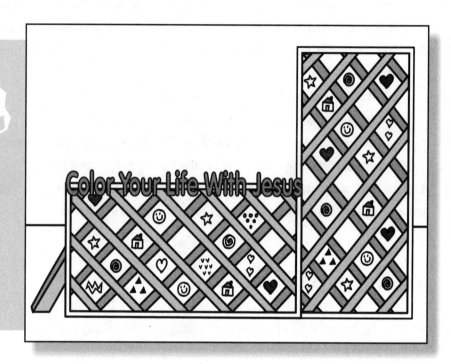

GET READY...

Be sure you have either purchased or cut out colorful letters to spell "Color Your Life With Jesus." Letters need to be at least 3" tall. Place the trellises and craft materials on a level floor.

GET SET...

Gather children and ask:

▶ **When is a time you invited people to a party? Why did you invite them?**

▶ **How did your guests feel at the party?**

▶ **Why is it important to share special celebrations?**

▶ **How is sharing Jesus with people like inviting them to a special celebration?**

Say: **Knowing, loving, and following Jesus is like a wonderful celebration. Loving Jesus makes us so happy that we want to share that joy with others. Even the Bible tells us to share the joy we have in Jesus!** Read aloud 1 Peter 1:8. Then ask:

▶ **Why is it important to share our joy in Jesus with others?**

▶ **How does sharing Jesus help other people? help us?**

16

▶ **In what ways can we share Jesus with others?**

Say: **Let's share our joy in Jesus with the entire church and with the whole community! We'll make a beautiful sculpture to display so everyone can share our special joy.**

GET CRAFTIN'...

Hand each child two sheets of construction paper or white paper. Set out a stack of colored construction paper and invite children to tear colorful scraps of paper to decorate their sheets of paper. Suggest torn paper flowers, rainbows, hearts, stars, and other designs to symbolize the joy of knowing, loving, and following Jesus. You may wish to play some lively, joyous music as children work.

When the sheets of paper are colorfully decorated, encourage children to hold up their designs and tell one reason they're glad they love Jesus. Then lay the wooden trellises flat on the floor and arrange the decorated sheets so portions of each design show through the latticework. Let children staple the papers in place along the wooden frames so the designs show through the latticework. When children are done stapling, run long pieces of clear packing tape across the backs of the papers to secure them to the trellises and to add stability.

Turn one of the trellises over and lay it flat on the ground. Let children sort the precut letters into the words "Color Your Life With Jesus." Arrange the letters across the long top edge of that trellis, keeping the wooden edge at the center of each letter. Staple the letters in place.

Let children cooperatively hold their projects and parade in and out of classrooms to share their joy—and beautiful artwork—with others. Then march outside and set the colorful creations next to a tree, sign, or bush so passersby can view the message. Tie the trellises together with string. If you plan to display the artwork each week, you may wish to ask an adult volunteer to construct a simple stand for the sculpture. (Be sure you display your project only on sunny days!) Children will feel delight when they drive by the church and view their important message of joy in Jesus.

Crafty Tips
▶ Display this special sculpture inside the church sanctuary to remind any down-in-the-dumps grown-ups that our joy comes from Jesus!

Crafty Tips
▶ Tie colorful helium balloons to the edges of the trellis to create more excitement and eye appeal.

Crazy Cars & Bodacious Boats

Come, follow me, Jesus said. Matthew 4:19

Bible Craft Concept
We want to follow Jesus.

Crafty Components
You'll need a Bible, paper plates, duct tape, glue sticks, markers, drinking straws, construction paper, cardboard tubes, scissors, and brass paper fasteners. You'll also need one medium- to large-sized box for every four children. The boxes should be large enough for one or two preschoolers to sit in.

GET READY...

Place the craft materials and boxes in the center of the room. Cut the end flaps off the tops of the boxes, then reinforce the box bottoms with duct tape. Make a photocopy of the action rhyme box from this activity.

GET SET...

Invite children to sit in a circle. Secretly choose one child to follow and imitate as he or she sits down. Then challenge all of the children to follow you as you stand, sit, pat your head, turn around, and sit down. Ask:

▶ **What does it mean to "follow" someone?**

▶ **Why might you decide to follow someone?**

▶ **Why do you think Jesus wants us to follow him?**

Say: **Following Jesus isn't always easy. Sometimes we follow Jesus by forgiving someone who's hard to forgive or by getting our chores done when we would rather play. But following Jesus is so very important. What good things happen when we follow Jesus?** Allow children to tell their ideas. Then ask a volunteer to read aloud Matthew 4:19. Ask:

▶ **Is there any time or any place we can't follow Jesus? Explain.**

▶ **In what ways can we follow Jesus more closely?**

Say: **Let's help teach some of our younger kids about following Jesus. We'll make gigantic cars and boats for them, then teach the children a fun rhyme about following Jesus.**

GET CRAFTIN'...

Form groups of four and assign each group a box. Let each group decide whether to sculpt a fancy boat or a cruisin' car. Use paper plates for car wheels and steering wheels on both cars and boats. Adding a brass paper fastener to the center of each "steering wheel" will allow it to turn. Use construction paper to make fancy dials, buttons, and other items such as CB radios, cellular phones, and speedometers. Paper triangles taped to drinking straws make fabulous boat flags, while drinking straws taped to cars work well for radio antennas. Let children's imaginations go wild—you'll be delighted with their creative inventions!

When the vehicles are complete, encourage children to visit each other's marvelous models. Then teach children the following action rhyme so they can teach it to the preschoolers in turn.

> We can follow Jesus anywhere we go:
> Zoom, car, zoom; row, boat, row!
> We can follow Jesus: putt, putt, vrooom!
> We can follow Jesus when we're going to the (fill in the blank)!
>
>

When your class is familiar with the rhyme, let them present the cars and boats to a class of preschoolers. Have your children tell the preschoolers how important it is to follow Jesus—and that we can follow Jesus anywhere. Have preschoolers "drive" their new cars and boats as your class teaches them the action rhyme. Present a photocopy of the rhyme to the preschool teacher so he or she can learn the action rhyme, too. End your time together by leading your class in singing "I Have Decided to Follow Jesus."

Crafty Tips

▶ For great sound effects, attach large jingle bells or inexpensive plastic bicycle horns to the pretend vehicles.

▶ To create truly mobile vehicles, you may wish to cut holes in the box bottoms for young children to stick their legs through.

Crafty Tips

▶ Join with another class to create a wider variety of vehicles such as airplanes, buses, tractors, fire engines, and trains. Have a parade for the congregation and explain why it's important to follow Jesus on land, sea, or sky—but especially in our hearts and lives!

Colossal Cuddle-Me Quilt

Your love, O Lord, reaches to the heavens. Psalm 36:5

Bible Craft Concept
God wraps us in his love.

Crafty Components
You'll need a Bible, fabric paints in squeeze bottles, paper, pencils, and a new white or light pastel twin-size blanket.

GET READY...

Before class, measure the blanket into equal-sized squares, making one square for each child in class. Use black fabric paint to trace the lines of the squares. Let the paint dry twenty-four hours.

Spread the blanket on the floor and smooth out any wrinkles. Place the remainder of the craft materials around the blanket.

GET SET...

Hug each child as you gather in a circle. Ask:

▶ **What does a hug feel like?**

▶ **What does a hug show?**

▶ **In what ways is a warm blanket like a cuddly hug?**

Say: **Cuddly hugs are one way to show someone our love. A hug makes us feel warm and good, safe and secure. When someone gives us a hug, it's like wrapping a big blanket of love and protection around us. How is God's love like a giant hug or a warm blanket?** Encourage children to tell their ideas. Then say: **Let's see what the Bible tells us about God's love.**

Ask several volunteers to read aloud Psalm 36:5-9. Then ask:

▶ **Why is it important to spread God's love to others?**

▶ **How can we spread God's warm love to others?**

Say: **God's love is like a special hug—a sweet blanket that covers us with God's protection and love. Let's make a giant blanket that we can give to someone to remind them that God wraps us in his love all the time.**

GET CRAFTIN'...

Hold up the blanket and point out the empty squares. Explain that each person will decorate one of the squares with colorful fabric paint. Have children form pairs, then hand each child a piece of paper and a pencil. Invite children to draw practice sketches of what they would like to draw in their squares. Encourage children to keep their pictures and designs very simple! Large stars, colorful hearts, cheery flowers, and wild geometric designs work well.

When you're ready to paint, begin with the top row of squares and work from left to right, allowing two children to paint their squares simultaneously. When all the squares have been decorated, slide the blanket into a "safety zone" where it won't be disturbed for twenty-four hours.

Next time children come to class, let them see and feel the quilt they made. To remind everyone that God wraps us in his love, invite each child or pair of children to wrap themselves in the blanket and to tell one way they feel God's love wrapped around them. Then have children brainstorm to whom they'd like to give the "cuddle-me quilt." Suggest an ill church member, an elderly person in the neighborhood, a homeless shelter, or a children's home. If possible, arrange for class members to present the quilt in person. Otherwise, be sure to take along a camera to capture the delighted smile of the recipient.

Crafty Tips

▶ This is a great whole-church craft project! Invite every Sunday school class, children's and adult, to participate. Have each class make a cuddle-me quilt to donate to a missionary your church supports.

Crafty Tips

▶ Decorated pillowcases make a great community service project. Decorate plain pillowcases with fabric paints, then donate the cheery creations to a children's hospital or nursing home.

Fantastic Fish & Loaves

And my God will meet all your needs. Philippians 4:19

Bible Craft Concept
God gives us what we need.

Crafty Components
You'll need a Bible, colored plastic garbage bags, newspapers, brown paper grocery sacks, tape, a laundry basket, construction paper, markers, and rubber bands or twist-tie wires.

GET READY...

Place the craft materials on the floor. Be sure you have plenty of newspapers to stuff the garbage bags and grocery sacks.

GET SET...

Gather children and ask:

▶ **What are the differences between needs and wants?**

▶ **What are some things that we need every day?**

▶ **Who gives us these things?**

▶ **What would happen if we didn't receive what we need?**

Say: **There are many things that we want and need. It's not so important to get the things we want, but it is important to have our needs met. Food, clothing, love, trust—all of these are important needs.**
Ask:

▶ **Can any one person supply all our needs? Explain.**

Say: **There is someone who can supply every need we have because he knows each of our needs even before we do! Who is that someone? God! Let's see what the Bible says about God giving us what we need.**

Ask a volunteer to read aloud Philippians 4:19. Then say: **We can trust God to supply what we need if we just pray and ask him. Remember the stories about Jesus feeding thousands? What did Jesus use to feed the people?** Pause for responses. **Jesus gave the people all the food they needed by feeding them with fish and loaves of bread. Even when it seemed impossible for someone to meet all those people's needs, Jesus did it. That's an important story to remember because it reminds us that God's Son, Jesus, will meet our needs, too. Let's make a giant fishy sculpture to remind us that Jesus gives us what we need.**

GET CRAFTIN'...

Have children form small groups. Hand each group a plastic garbage bag and a pile of newspapers. Explain that these will be made into giant squishy-fish by stuffing the bags with newspapers. Tell children to stuff their bags fairly full but to leave about 10" at the open end of the bags. Then close the end of the bags with rubber bands or twist-tie wires to make "fish tails."

Use colorful construction paper to make fins, eyes, mouths, scales, and other designs on the fish. Tape the festive features in place. Set the fish aside.

To make the loaves, have each group stuff a brown paper grocery sack with newspapers. Then fold down the top edges and tape them to the bag. Gently squish the "bread" into loaf shapes. Use brown markers to draw "loaf lines" across the top of each paper loaf. Place the loaves in the laundry basket. For a special touch, weave strips of construction paper or crepe paper in and out of the openings in the basket.

Decide where you'd like to display your unusual sculpture. Then stack the giant fish one on top of the other or any other way you desire. Place the basket with the paper loaves beside the fish. If you would like, add a Scripture sign with Philippians 4:19 written on it to remind others that all our needs are met in Jesus.

Crafty Tips

▶ Keep the fish and loaves to help act out the story of Jesus' miracle for a younger class.

▶ Donate the fish to a preschool room and let delighted children take a "ride" on the backs of the fish as they scoot around the room.

Crafty Tips

▶ Use the fish in a church carnival game. Tape a number on the bottom of each fish. Then let young children toss green beanbag "worms" at the "sea" of fish. Award children the same number of tickets or Gummi Worms as the fish the worm lands closest to.

Built on Giant Love

I am going there to prepare a place for you. John 14:2

Bible Craft Concept
Jesus is preparing our heavenly home.

Crafty Components
You'll need a Bible, construction paper, markers, scissors, clear packing tape, sandpaper, fishing line or yarn, brown paper grocery sacks, and three very large boxes.

GET READY...

Cut the flaps off the open ends of the boxes. Save the flaps to use as signs. Use clear packing tape to reinforce the seams of the boxes. If you do not have older children in class, you may wish to cut out the door and window shapes before class. Use scissors or a knife to cut the openings.

Set the boxes in different areas of the room. Place the craft materials in the center of the room for everyone to share.

GET SET...

Gather children in a group. Ask:

▶ **What is something you had to prepare for?**

▶ **Why is preparation so important?**

Say: **Jesus said that he is preparing us a new home in heaven. In what ways is preparing a new house similar to Jesus preparing us a home in heaven?** Encourage children to share their ideas. Then say: **Preparing a home or a building takes a lot of planning, thought, care, and even love. Just think of the love that Jesus is putting into our heavenly home! You know, there are many homes and buildings in the Bible, but none is as wonderful as the home Jesus is making for us. Let's read about the time Jesus**

promised to prepare for us a special home.

Ask volunteers to take turns reading aloud John 14:1, 2. Then ask:

▶ **How does preparing for something or someone show our love?**

Say: **Isn't it wonderful that Jesus is preparing a special place for us? We can prepare special places, too! They can remind us that even though many homes and buildings are mentioned in the Bible, the best home of all is the one Jesus is preparing for us in heaven!**

GET CRAFTIN'...

Form three groups and assign each group a box. Explain that the boxes will be used to make neat buildings or houses like the ones that may have been built during Jesus' time. Have one group build an inn like the one in the story of Jesus' birth. Have a second group construct a market or store, such as might have been found along the streets of Jerusalem. Have the third group create a house such as the one where Jesus raised the centurion's daughter or where the last supper was shared. Use the following suggestions to get you started, then let the children's imaginations run free!

▶ **The Inn**—Use sandpaper for tactile stones on the front of the building. Use a cardboard flap to make a sign saying "INN" and attach it to the building. You may wish to glue strips of yellow construction paper or even real straw or hay to the roof.

▶ **The Market**—Make a scalloped border out of colorful paper and tape it to the top edge of the building as an "awning." Prepare a sign from a cardboard flap that says "MARKET." Attach the sign above the door. Cut or tear out construction paper "foods" such as fish, fruit, or vegetables. Hang them in the doorway with fishing line or yarn. Cover the sides of the building with brown paper grocery bag "stones."

▶ **The House**—Tear out brown paper stones and tape or glue them to the front and sides of the building. You may wish to add bits of sandpaper to the stones for a more realistic effect. Suggest adding a box "table" inside the house or a paper "wall-hanging" on the inside wall.

When the buildings are complete, have a "Parade of Homes" and tour the creative architecture. Then donate the super-city to another class. Younger children will enjoy hours of fun as they play in these tactile buildings and pretend they're in Jerusalem with Jesus!

Crafty Tips
▶ Use these adorable abodes for skit props (the Inn is great at Christmas!), VBS or church carnival decorations, playhouses, or any time you want a snappy special effect.

Crafty Tips
▶ The more tactile embellishments you use, the better! Try using grass cloth wallpaper for walls, rolled cork for roofs, and corrugated bulletin board paper for textured "bricks." Real fabric for curtains and awnings is a great touch!

Clean As a Whistle

Serve one another in love. Galatians 5:13

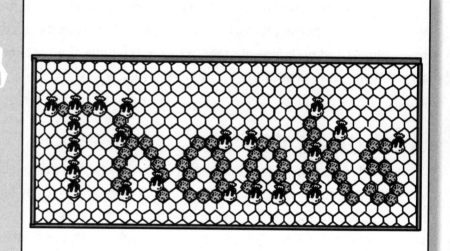

Bible Craft Concept
We can serve others.

Crafty Components
You'll need a Bible, a wooden trellis, a stapler, one disposable cloth towelette for each child, soap flakes, rubber bands, tape, sponges, paper towels, and various lengths of ribbon. You'll also need enough chicken wire to cover the trellis on one side.

GET READY...

Before class, cut the chicken wire so it covers one side of the wooden trellis. Staple the wire over the frame of the trellis. Cut each disposable cloth in half.

GET SET...

Form small groups. Say: **Let's play a game of Serving Charades. I'll whisper an action such as washing dishes to one group. Then that group will act out the charade, and the rest of you can guess what is being acted out.**

Use these suggestions for Serving Charades: helping someone up after he or she has fallen, tying someone's shoes, serving dinner to someone, and praying with someone. When everyone has had a chance to act out a charade, ask:

▶ **What did all these actions have in common?**

▶ **How was each action a good example of serving others?**

▶ **Why do you think Jesus wants us to serve one another?**

Say: **Jesus taught us to serve one another to show our love for them—and to show our love for Jesus. Did you know that Jesus served his disciples in a very important way? In Jesus' time, it was polite to** wash your guests' dusty feet. Washing your guests' feet showed you were willing to serve them. Let's read about the special time Jesus served his friends. Have children take turns reading aloud John 13:1-16. Then ask:

▶ **In what way did washing his friends' feet show Jesus' love for them?**

▶ **How can serving others demonstrate our love for them? for Jesus?**

▶ **In what ways can we serve others?**

Read aloud Galatians 5:13, then say: **We're to serve others in kindness and in love. Let's lovingly serve someone in our community. We'll make a special sculpture sign to say thank-you to them—and to remind us how Jesus washed the disciples' feet and served them with love.**

Crafty Tips

▶ Invite another class to join in your community service efforts so you can make festive trellises for police officers and firefighters to clean their dusty vehicles.

GET CRAFTIN'...

Hand each child two disposable cloths and two rubber bands. Show children how to pour a small handful of soap flakes into the center of each cloth and then bring the edges up and fasten the ends with a rubber band to make a "soap sachet."

Have children help cut the sponges into 4" squares. Then help children poke the ends of the sachets, the sponges, and paper towels into the holes in the chicken wire to spell out "THANKS." Use double rows of sachets, sponges, and paper towels to make the letters. Then tape or tie ribbon to the trellis to make it flashy and fun.

As children work, explain that the soap sachets will be used to wash dishes and to clean tables in a homeless shelter. The soap flakes will suds up when they're emptied into a tub of water, and the disposable cloths, sponges, and paper towels can be used to make cleanup a snap!

Decide whom you would like to present your crafty gift to, then arrange a time for the presentation of your special "trellis of love." Be sure to explain to the recipients how the sachets, sponges, and paper towels work.

Crafty Tips

▶ Make this special trellis for the church staff, then arrange a time for the class to pitch in and wash their cars.

Mega-Map of Bible Lands

But as for you, continue in what you have learned. 2 Timothy 3:14

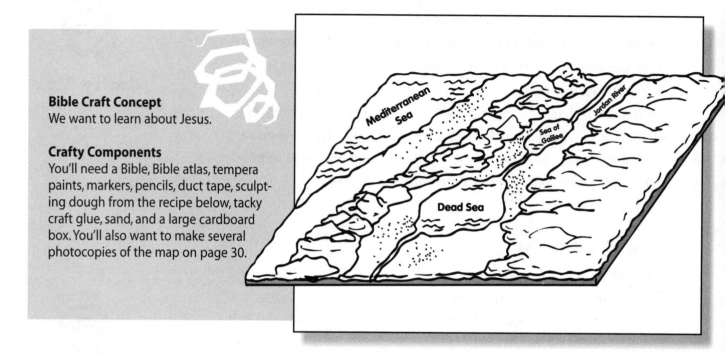

Bible Craft Concept
We want to learn about Jesus.

Crafty Components
You'll need a Bible, Bible atlas, tempera paints, markers, pencils, duct tape, sculpting dough from the recipe below, tacky craft glue, sand, and a large cardboard box. You'll also want to make several photocopies of the map on page 30.

GET READY...

Flatten the box and cut off its end flaps so a cardboard square or rectangle remains. Make sure that the long sides of the remaining piece are at least 3' long. Tape the back of the cardboard with duct tape in a criss-cross pattern to support the map once the sculpting dough is added.

Prepare a batch of sculpting dough by mixing 3 cups salt, 1 cup baking soda, and 1 cup water. Add several drops of blue, red, and green food coloring to give the dough a brownish tint. Knead the dough until it is pliable but gritty. Store the dough in an airtight plastic bag for up to one week.

Set the craft materials on a hard floor. You may wish to spread newspapers under the work area.

GET SET...

Have kids get into pairs or trios. Then invite children each to tell their groups where they're from and one interesting hobby they have. When everyone has had a turn to share the information, gather children and ask:

▶ **How does knowing where someone is from help you know that person better?**

▶ **Why is it important to learn about others? about Jesus?**

Say: **We want to learn as much as we can about Jesus so we can understand and follow him more closely. Knowing where Jesus was born and where he grew up helps us understand more about him.**

For example, we know from the Bible that Jesus walked many places to teach and help people. But where did he go? How far did he walk? What was the land like? To learn more about Jesus and his ministry, let's see what the Bible says about the different places Jesus lived and visited.

Ask children to share Bibles as they look together through Matthew, Mark, Luke, and John. Challenge children to search for the names of places, towns, and rivers that Jesus visited. After several minutes of searching, ask volunteers to read the names they found.

Then hold up a map of Palestine during the time Jesus lived. (Use a map from the Bible atlas, your Bible, or the photocopies of the map on page 30.) Let children point to the places they found in the Bible. Then say: **There's an even better way to find out more about the places Jesus lived. We can make a mega-map to help us learn more about Jesus.**

GET CRAFTIN'...

Have several children use photocopies of the map to sketch an outline of Palestine during the life of Jesus on the cardboard. Have other children look at the Bible atlas or photocopies of the map to find out where the mountainous region should be located (between the Mediterranean Sea and the Jordan River). Use sculpting dough to build up mountains in those areas of the map.

Let children use blue paint or markers to color the Jordan River, Sea of Galilee, Mediterranean Sea, and Dead Sea. Have other children paint or color both sides of the Jordan River green. The coastlines can be green with a bit of sand glued to the "beaches" of the Mediterranean Sea and the two inland seas.

When the map is dry, have children use a fine-tipped marker to label the cities and bodies of water.

Use this tactile relief map to enhance your studies of Jesus and the areas in which he lived and ministered to others. Encourage children to share this learning tool with other classes and to explain some of the key points labeled on the map. You may wish to assign pairs simple research projects to learn more about the places on the map. Then allow partners to use the map as a learning prop as they share their information with the entire class.

Crafty Tips

▶ To create a map with greater durability and stability, use a large piece of plywood or fiberboard as the base of your mega-map. It will travel easily from room to room and allow lots of learning for lots of kids!

Crafty Tips

▶ Have older children do a bit of research to determine the distances between towns and seas. Then create your map according to a scale of one inch for every four miles.

Mega-Map of Bible Lands

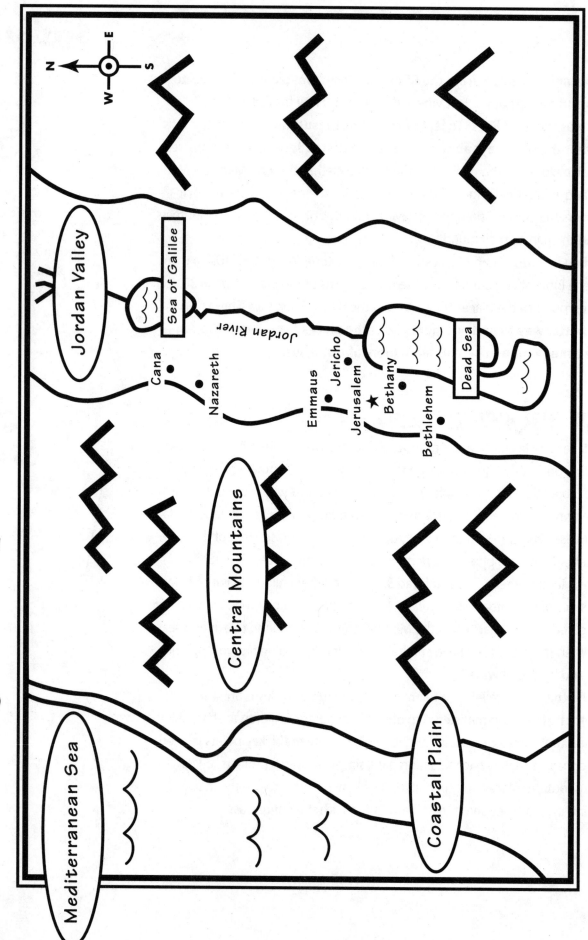

Chapter 2

GIGANTIC GAMES

Dominating dominoes, tremendous tic-tac-toe, mammoth candy tag, fabulous funky phones—and a treasure-trove more!

Hop to It!

Jonah obeyed the word of the Lord and went to Nineveh. Jonah 3:3

Bible Craft Concept
When God says "Go!" we hop to it.

Crafty Components
You'll need a Bible, colored construction paper, permanent markers, tape, rubber bands, two old pillowcases, newspapers, and two green or brown trash bags.

GET READY...

Set out the craft materials.

GET SET...

Have children hop to form a circle. Then say: **Let's pretend we're frogs on lily pads while we play a crazy game of Froggy Says. Follow my directions and do exactly what Froggy says. But whenever I say, "Hop, hop," take two hops to your right. If you don't follow the directions and "hop to it," you must go to the center of the pond. Ready?**

Play this game like Simon Says. Supplement the directions below with your own—but be sure to give several commands to "Hop, hop" as you play.

▶ **Froggy says, "Croak like a frog."**

▶ **Froggy says, "Wave to a frog across the pond."**

▶ **Froggy says, "Twirl around on your lily pad."**

▶ **Froggy says, "Catch a pretend fly on your tongue."**

After you've played several minutes, say: **Froggy says, "Sit down on your lily pads."** Then ask:

▶ **Why did you follow my directions so carefully?**

▶ **When did you hop to it?**

▶ **What might have happened if you hadn't hopped when I said to?**

Say: **In this game, if you didn't hop to it, you were out! I'm glad this was only a game, aren't you? But did you know that God gives us commands to move in real life? When God tells us to do something, we want to hop to it!** Ask:

▶ **When is a time you did something for God?**

▶ **Why do you think it's important to hop to it when God tells us to do something?**

▶ **What might happen if we don't get moving and follow God?**

Say: **Long ago God told Jonah to hop to it, but he didn't! What happened to Jonah?** Pause for children to tell the story of Jonah and the big fish. Then ask a volunteer to read aloud Jonah 3:1-3. Say: **Jonah learned that it's important to go when God says to go. Let's make a fun game to remind another class to hop to it when God says "Go!"**

Crafty Tips

▶ Make individual frogs by stuffing green party bags or lunch sacks with newspapers. Then play Hop to It with a whole pond full of croakers!

Crafty Tips

▶ Play a crazy game of Froggy Volleyball. Place the lily pads on the ground as a "net," then volley the fat froggies back and forth.

GET CRAFTIN'...

Form two groups and have each group make a giant frog and lily pad. Make the frogs by stuffing wadded newspapers into the plastic bags, then securing the ends of the bags with rubber bands. Be sure your "frogs" are plump! Create construction paper features such as eyes, freckles, warts, webbed feet, and big smiles. Tape the paper features to the frogs. Make lily pads by coloring green, white, and yellow flowers on the pillowcases.

When kids are finished, have them play Hop to It. Have the two groups stand on opposite sides of the playing area. Have one group place its frog on the lily pad and then, holding the edges of the lily pad, vault the frog toward the other team. The opposing team must try to catch the froggy as it leaps in the air! Award one point for each successful froggy catch. Play until one group scores five points. Then donate the giant game to another class and remind them how important it is to hop to it when God says "Go!"

Go, Go! Tic-Tac-Toe!

They must obey God's commands and keep their faith in Jesus. Revelation 14:12 (ICB)

Bible Craft Concept
Where we place our faith is important.

Crafty Components
You'll need a Bible, permanent markers, a yardstick, paper plates, and one solid-colored shower curtain liner.

GET READY...
Place the craft materials on a hard level floor.

GET SET...
Gather children around the craft materials. Hold the permanent markers in one hand a few inches above the floor. Let the markers drop, then challenge children to pick up one marker at a time without disturbing any of the other markers. When each marker has been collected, ask:

▶ **Why did you choose to pick up certain markers?**

▶ **What if you had snatched a marker from under another one?**

Say: **Just as you were careful to choose the place you picked up a marker, we need to be careful of the places we choose to put our faith and trust. If we put our faith or trust in the wrong things or people, we might lose!** Ask:

▶ **What are things we don't want to put our faith in?** Encourage children to name things such as money, the weather, false teachers, and the world in general.

▶ **Where are some of the right places to put our faith?** Help children name the Bible, Jesus, God, God's truth, and God's Word.

▶ **How do we know when our faith is in the right place? the wrong place?**

Ask a volunteer to read aloud Revelation 14:12. Then say: **Just as we choose our moves carefully in the games we play, we must choose carefully where to place our faith. When our faith is in the right place with God, we will win every time! We can make a great game to donate to the church for picnics and get-togethers. And the best part is that this game will remind everyone how important it is to make the right move of placing our faith in God.**

GET CRAFTIN'...

Spread the shower curtain liner on the floor and smooth out any wrinkles. Have children use the yardstick and markers to draw a large, thick tic-tac-toe outline on the liner. Encourage children to decorate the borders of the curtain with colorful designs and the slogan: "Choose carefully where to place YOUR faith!" Ask several children to color giant Os and Xs on paper plates. Make five plates with each letter.

To play, form two teams, the Xs and the Os. Hand each group its paper plates, then let group members take turns holding the plates and choosing carefully where to stand on the game grid. Score one point each time a group makes a tic-tac-toe. For real learning fun, ask Bible-trivia or Bible-story questions that groups must answer correctly before they're allowed to choose a place to stand!

Crafty Tips
▶ Make rows of large dots on the reverse side of the shower curtain liner, then let teams use erasable crayons to draw lines between the dots as they answer Bible-related questions. When the lines are drawn to complete boxes, have group members write their initials in the boxes.

Crafty Tips
▶ Take this giant game mat on picnics for giant fun.
▶ This delightful game mat works for beanbag toss games at church carnivals or holiday get-togethers.

Mammoth Candy Tag

Teach them to obey everything that I have told you. Matthew 28:20 (ICB)

Bible Craft Concept
We can tell others about Jesus.

Crafty Components
You'll need a Bible, scissors, newspapers, stapler, clear packing tape, black marker, pencils, and two large sheets each of red, blue, yellow, green, and orange poster board. You'll also want a bag of small wrapped candies.

GET READY...

Before class, make poster board patterns of mammoth round, oval, and oblong candies. Make the pattern as large as possible by rounding the corners of a large sheet of poster board. Then set the pattern and other craft materials on the floor.

GET SET...

Gather children around the craft materials. Hold up the bag of candy. Say: **Let's play a different game of Chain Tag. I'll be It. If I tag you, I'll hand you a candy and whisper a sweet message in your ear. Then you can hold your candy as you help me tag others and tell them the message. We'll play until everyone has a piece of candy and has heard the sweet message.** When someone is tagged, whisper, "Jesus loves you." When everyone has heard the message, have kids nibble their candies and ask:

▶ **What was the sweet message you heard?**

▶ **How did we spread this important message?**

▶ **How is telling others about Jesus like a game of Chain Tag?**

Say: **The game of Chain Tag starts with one person but ends with everyone tagged or bound together. That's how it is when we tell others about Jesus. One person starts the message by telling others, who** spread that message. Pretty soon, lots of people have heard about Jesus and are bound together in love!

▶ **How does telling others about Jesus help them? help us?**

▶ **Who can you tell about Jesus this week?**

Have a volunteer read aloud Matthew 28:19, 20. Then say: **Jesus wants us to tell others about his love and how he died for us so we can become God's friends. Just like a special game of Chain Tag, we can tell as many people as possible about Jesus! Let's make a great game to remind others about the importance of sharing Jesus.**

GET CRAFTIN'...

Have children form five groups. Hand each group two sheets of the same color of poster board. Explain that children are going to make mammoth paper candies to use in a game. Have children use the patterns to trace large circles, ovals, or oblong shapes on their sheets of poster board, then cut them out. Show children how to staple the edges of their paper candies about two-thirds of the way around. Then instruct children to wad newspapers and stuff the paper candies until they're plump. Finish stapling the edges, then cover the staples with clear packing tape. Use the marker to draw candy sprinkles or peppermint stripes on the top of each paper candy.

Then use one of the mammoth candies to play Toss-Across Chain Tag. Hand one paper candy to five children. Explain that only kids holding the giant candy can tag someone. Tagged players must help hold the giant candy and help tag others. Play until everyone has been tagged. For a fun variation, go outside and play Colossal Candy Frisbee-Toss. Have children scatter around the play area and take turns sailing the colossal candies back and forth as they name ways to tell others about Jesus. For an extra sweet time, take these colorful candies on church retreats.

Crafty Tips

▶ Hang these colossal candies from the ceiling to make a mammoth mobile. Make a title card that reads "Candies for the sweet tooth—JESUS for the sweet truth!" to hang in the middle of the display.

Crafty Tips

▶ Play a giant game of Heads or Tails with the paper candies. Or pass the colossal candies in zany ways for relay races.

Dominating Dominoes

For now we really live, since you are standing firm in the Lord. 1 Thessalonians 3:8

Bible Craft Concept
We can stand up for God.

Crafty Components
You'll need a Bible, permanent markers, clear tape, newspapers, and ten large white gift boxes. Gift boxes that are made for blankets, shirts, sweaters, or bathrobes work well.

GET READY...

Set out the craft materials and boxes.

GET SET...

Gather children and say: **Let's play a game. I'll ask a question, then you signal your answer by standing up if you agree or by sitting down if you disagree. Ready? The sun is hot.** Pause for children to signal their responses. **Rocks are hard.** Pause. **Chocolate ice cream is best.** Pause. **School is fun.** Pause. **Clouds are as heavy as mountains.** When all the children are seated in response, ask:

▶ **Why did some of you stand on a particular question while others sat?**

▶ **How did you decide whether to stand up for something?**

Say: **When people stand up for someone or something, it means they believe in that person or thing and won't change their minds—even if someone tries to make them. Who are people you stand up for?** Give children time to tell their ideas. Then ask:

▶ **Why is it important to stand up for God?**

▶ **What happens when we don't stand up for God?**

Say: **Think about a line of dominoes standing up on their edges. What happens when something** comes along to push one over? They all fall down! That's how it is with us. People may try to tell us that God isn't big or powerful. They may try to topple us like you would topple a row of dominoes. But if we stand up for God, we won't fall over! We can help each other stand up for God so our friends won't topple over, either.

▶ **How can you show others you stand up for God?**

▶ **How can we help ourselves stand for God? help others stand for God?**

Read aloud 1 Thessalonians 3:8, then say: **Let's make a set of dynamite dominoes to remind us how important it is to stand up for God. Then we'll give the dominoes to another class to remind them to stand up for God, too.**

GET CRAFTIN'...

Form ten small groups, each of which will make a domino. If your class is small, form five groups and have each group make two dominoes. Have groups use wadded newspapers to "stuff" their boxes to make them sturdier, then tape the edges closed. Use a marker to draw a line dividing each box into two halves like the two ends of a domino. Then draw sets of dots on the box halves to resemble actual dominoes. Use numbers from one to six. Do the same for the back of each box, but use different number combinations.

To play, form two groups and place the dominoes in a pile. Ask one group a Bible-based question to review a recent Bible story or lesson. If that group answers correctly, let them lay a domino flat on the floor. Then ask the next group a question. If they answer correctly, have them lay a matching domino next to the first one. Continue play until there are no more usable dominoes. For a fun finale, invite one group to stand the dominoes on their edges, then have the other group start a chain reaction topple. Donate the huge dominoes to another class and explain why it's important to stand up for God.

Crafty Tips
▶ Use this humongous set of dominoes as obstacles for relay races.

Crafty Tips
▶ For a fun game of Number Bowling, set up the dominoes and bowl them over with a playground ball. Count the numbers on the pins left standing. Lowest score gets to choose the next game.

Super "Sea-Saw"

We wait in hope for the Lord; he is our help and our shield. Psalm 33:20

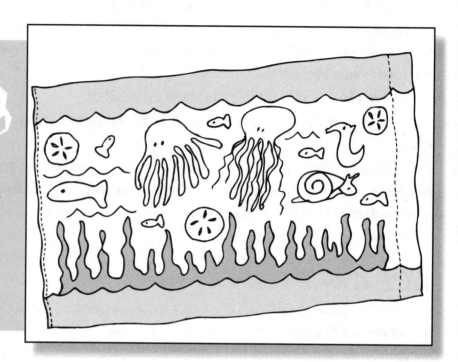

Bible Craft Concept
God helps us.

Crafty Components
You'll need a Bible, tacky craft glue, scissors, sandpaper, pencils, thick white tempera paint, blue chalk, blue and silver sequins, and shimmery blue fabric such as satin. You'll also need an old white or blue bedsheet, markers, construction paper, and balloons.

GET READY...

Before class, cut out a sandpaper starfish and a blue satin fish, jellyfish, or seashell. Spread the bedsheet on the floor and place the craft materials around the edges. You may wish to put newspapers under the sheet if you're working on carpet.

GET SET...

Gather children and say: **There are lots of stories in the Bible about lakes, water, and splashing seas. What are some of those stories?** Encourage children to name stories such as Jonah, Noah, Moses crossing the Red Sea, and Jesus calming the storm. Then say: **All the stories you named have one important thing in common—they're all about how God helped the people he loved. All through the Bible, we learn about God's help and loving care.** Ask:

▶ **Why do you think God helps us?**

▶ **How does God help in your life?**

Say: **God's help is like a special gift we can trust to always be there. Let's see what the Bible says about God's help.** Have several volunteers read aloud Psalms 33:20; 121:1, 2; and Hebrews 13:6. Then say: **Because God loves us, he wants us to remember that he helps us—just as he helped Moses, Noah, and**

Jonah. We can help the younger children remember God's help, too. We'll make them a beautiful pretend ocean to play with as they remember how God helped Moses, Noah, and Jonah—and how God helps us, too.

GET CRAFTIN'...

Point to the bedsheet and explain that the sheet is a pretend sea. Challenge children to think of all the beautiful things they might see in the ocean, such as sandy starfish, round sand dollars, colorful seashells, and oodles of fish. Hold up the sandpaper starfish and satin fish, jellyfish, or seashell. Challenge children to use the sandpaper and blue satin to create sea creatures and then glue them to the bedsheet. Use sequins to add shimmery effects to the ocean. Show children how to dip the chalk into the thick tempera paint and draw ocean waves and ripples over the bedsheet.

As the wondrous sea scene dries, invite children to make balloon fish by blowing up and tying off colorful balloons. Then have children tear paper fins and scales from construction paper and tape them to the "fish." Use markers to add googly eyes and fishy smiles. Then teach children the following rhyme, which they can teach to a class of younger children.

> **Moses crossed the Red Sea, Red Sea, Red Sea.**
> **Moses crossed the Red Sea—what did he see?**
> **Moses saw a blue fish, blue fish, blue fish.**
> **Moses saw a blue fish—what else did he see?**
> *(Continue with other colors.)*

Have children hold the bedsheet around the edges and place the balloon fish beside them. Then, as they repeat the action rhyme, have them wiggle and wave the pretend sea and add appropriate fish as colors are named. Make the fish swim and swish in the pretend sea! Donate the "super sea" and balloon fish to a younger classroom and teach them the "Moses" rhyme. Other verses to teach younger children might include: "Noah sailed the big flood" and "Jonah swam the blue sea."

Crafty Tips

▶ Donate this playful ocean to a younger children's classroom, then invite older and younger children to repeat the action rhyme together.

Crafty Tips

▶ Use this creative craft as a huge hanging wall mural when you study Noah, Jonah, Jesus calming the storm, or Moses crossing the Red Sea.

Colossal Willie Worm

From him the whole body, joined and held together...builds itself up in love.
Ephesians 4:16

Bible Craft Concept
We can join together for Jesus!

Crafty Components
You'll need a Bible, two tennis balls, permanent markers, fiberfill, duct tape or packing tape, rubber bands, and ten or more pairs of clean, old socks (adult sizes).

GET READY...

Colorful tube socks or knee socks with interesting patterns work best for this unique craft idea. Sockless? Check out thrift stores for next-to-nothing prices or hold a church sock drive.

GET SET...

Gather children and say: **When I call out a number, run to link elbows with others to make a group of that size. Ready? Three!** Continue calling out numbers and having kids form groups. Call numbers quickly to keep the game moving and to challenge players. After several rounds, gather kids and ask:

▶ **How can joining with others help us spread the good news about Jesus? help us spread Jesus' love?**

▶ **Why do you think Jesus wants us to join with others in our faith?**

▶ **Who are people you join with to spread Jesus' love?** Lead children to mention their families, church groups, and friends.

Say: **Let's see what the Bible tells us about joining with others in Jesus' name.** Ask several volunteers to read aloud the following verses: Ephesians 4:16; Galatians 3:26-28; and Ephesians 4:4-6. Then say: **Joining with other Christians is not only a good way to share Jesus' love and spread his love to others, it's also fun! Let's join together right now and make a fun game to share with others in our church.**

GET CRAFTIN'...

Form two groups. Give each group ten unmatched socks, a large pile of fiberfill, and a tennis ball. Have each group place a tennis ball into the toe of one sock and twist rubber bands around the sock to make a "head." Encourage children to draw facial features on the heads to make cheery Willie Worms. Then show groups how to stuff fiberfill into the socks, leaving about 2" unstuffed near the ankle opening. Help children tape the ankle of the stuffed sock to the toe of another sock. Make sure to wrap the tape around the socks several times. (See illustration below.) Continue stuffing and taping socks until each group has joined all ten socks together into a long stuffed "worm." As you work, visit about how we can encourage others to join together for Jesus and what good things come to us when we're joined with Christ.

Crafty Tips
► Invite children to use markers and colored electrical tape to decorate the Willie Worms.

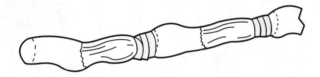

When the two Willie Worms are finished, play the following outdoor games.

► **Join-Together Tag.** One person holds Willie Worm by the head and runs to tag other players. When a player is tagged, he or she holds the next section of the worm, and the two players try to tag others. Keep adding players until there are no more worm segments to hold. If your group is large, use both Willie Worms. Reminder: Tell kids not to tug too hard on Willie—or you'll have to do minor surgery with more tape!

► **Willie Jump-Overs.** Hold Willie Worm by the end of the tail and twirl the head around in a circle several inches above the ground. Players hop, step, or jump over Willie each time he circles around. If a player misses, he or she becomes the next Twirler. For an extra challenge, twirl two Willie Worms in opposite directions.

► **Willie Toss-Ups.** Choose one person to hold Willie and then toss him high in the air as the other players run to scatter. When Willie is caught, players must freeze in place. The player holding Willie takes five giant steps and tries to tag someone by tossing Willie at his or her feet.

When you're finished playing, donate the Willie Worms to another classroom or to the church to use on picnics and family retreats.

Crafty Tips
► Toss Willie in the car or van for the next church outing or picnic.

Humongous Helpful Hopscotch

Share with God's people who are in need. Romans 12:13

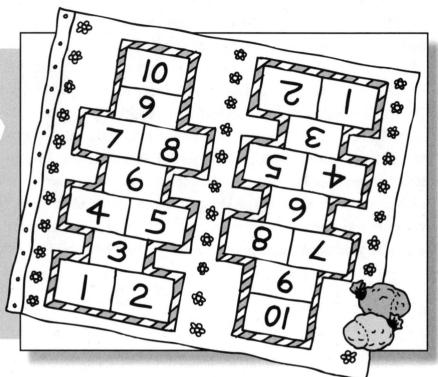

Bible Craft Concept
God wants us to help each other.

Crafty Components
You'll need a Bible, permanent markers, a solid-color shower curtain liner, a yardstick, tacky craft glue, felt, scissors, duct tape, a bag of uncooked rice, and two old socks.

GET READY...

Before class, use permanent markers and a yardstick to draw the outlines of two hopscotch boards on the shower curtain liner. Make sure the hopscotch boards face in opposite directions. (See illustration on opposite page.) Be sure there's about 1' of space between the outlines. Do not add numbers or designs to the giant game boards.

GET SET...

Have children get into pairs. Hand each child three grains of rice. Challenge children to scatter the rice around them on the floor, then pick up the rice while standing on one foot. When every grain of rice is gathered, repeat the activity but this time have partners hold each other's hands or arms as they pick up all the rice. Then ask:

▶ **Which was easier: picking up the rice alone or with help? Explain.**

▶ **What are other things that are easier to do when we have help?**

▶ **Why does God want us to help one another?**

Say: **In many Bible stories, we read about people helping each other. Ruth helped Naomi by gathering grain to eat. Jonathan helped David escape the mean king. And Moses helped God's people cross**

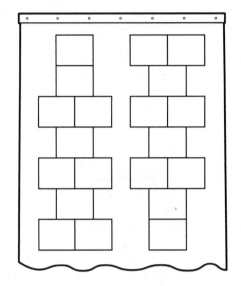

the Red Sea. Without help, some things wouldn't be possible. God helps us every day, and he wants us to be ready to help others, too. Ask a volunteer to read aloud Romans 12:13. Then ask:

▶ **How does helping others bring us closer to God?**

▶ **What are ways to help others?**

▶ **Who can you help this week?**

Say: **We can help another class right now! We'll make a huge helping hopscotch game to help them learn how important it is to help others.**

GET CRAFTIN'...

Form three groups. Have two groups work on the hopscotch boards while the third group makes two colorful beanbags. To make the beanbags, have children fill each sock half full of uncooked rice, then tightly knot the ankle of each sock. Cut off the sock material about 1" above the knot. Cut colorful felt shapes and glue them to the socks.

To make the hopscotch boards, spread the shower curtain liner on a hard floor and tape it securely in place. Let children use markers to add numbers to each box. Write "1" in the bottom left-hand corner of each board, "2" in the box beside it, and so on until each game has been numbered to ten. Invite children to draw colorful designs on the liner or to make rainbow stripes around the numbered boxes.

To play, form two teams and have each stand at the beginning of its board. Play the game the same as traditional hopscotch. Have player one on each team toss a beanbag to box 1, hop to retrieve it, and then hop to the end of the board and back. Players on opposite teams must help each other by holding hands or linking arms as they bend down to retrieve their beanbags. Continue playing until children on each team have hopped to box 10 and back.

Donate the game to another class and explain the importance of helping one another. Then join that class in a rousing game of Helpful Hopscotch!

Crafty Tips

▶ Turn over the shower curtain liner and draw a large four-square box. Use a playground ball to play four-square, dodge ball, or a variety of other traditional games.

Raucous Roll-Overs

The Lord your God will be with you wherever you go. Joshua 1:9

Bible Craft Concept
We can't hide from God.

Crafty Components
You'll need a Bible, colored electrical tape, crepe paper, scissors, and two very large, new plastic waste cans.

GET READY...

Purchase huge plastic waste cans from any discount store or hardware center. Remember: These sturdy crafts will provide hours and hours of giggly fun for many children! Before class, use shears or a sharp knife to cut the bottoms from the waste cans.

GET SET...

Have children play a quick game of Hide and Seek around the room or playing area. Then gather kids in a group and ask:

▶ **Is it possible to hide from other people? Explain.**

▶ **Is it possible to hide from God? Why or why not?**

Say: **In the Bible, we learn about Jonah and how God used a great fish to teach Jonah a lot of lessons. But one of the biggest lessons he learned was that we can't hide from God! God sees us wherever we are and knows what we're up to. Why do you think God wants to know where we are?** Let children explain their answers. Then read aloud Joshua 1:9 and Psalm 139:7-10. Ask:

▶ **Do you think it's good that God sees us all the time? Why or why not?**

Say: **Because God loves us, he wants to see us all the time. Like Jonah, we may try to hide from God,**

but God can't be fooled. He sees us anywhere we are! Let's make fun "Roll-Overs" to play with and to remind others that God sees us all the time.

GET CRAFTIN'...

Form two groups. Give each group a plastic waste can. Invite children to use colorful electrical tape to decorate their "Hide and Seek" Roll-Overs. Suggest bright stars, flowers, stripes, or other geometric designs. Then have children tear various lengths of crepe paper and tape the streamers around the openings on the waste cans.

Use the festive Roll-Overs to play the following fun games.

▶ Play Peek-n-Seek by letting children take turns hiding in the Roll-Overs and guessing who's inside.

▶ Play In, Out, Round-About by choosing different children to lead the others in crawling, scooching, or wriggling in and out of the Roll-Overs, forward and backward—or rolling over the sides of the barrels on their tummies. Remember: the faster the funnier!

▶ Stand the Roll-Overs upright at opposite ends of a large playing area, then play a lively game of field basketball.

▶ Use the barrels at a carnival for beanbag tosses or other games of skill.

When you're finished playing, donate the Roll-Overs to the church or to another classroom. Invite others to invent new ways to "get the fun rolling" while they remember that we can't hide from God.

Crafty Tips
▶ Store the Roll-Overs in empty rooms or closets where they'll make sturdy broom and mop holders.

Crafty Tips
▶ Add these safe, colorful barrels to your church playground or toddler room.

The Tremendous "Telephose"

The Lord will hear when I call to him. Psalm 4:3

Bible Craft Concept
God hears us when we talk to him.

Crafty Components
You'll need a Bible, acrylic paints and brushes, 16-ounce plastic drinking cups, newspapers, duct tape, and scissors. You'll also need several old garden hoses.

GET READY...

Before class, cut the garden hoses into 3' or 4' sections. Make sure you have two plastic cups for each section of hose. Cut a hole in the bottom of each plastic cup just large enough for the end of the hose to go through.

GET SET...

Seat children in a circle. Play a traditional game of Telephone by whispering a short message in someone's ear, having that person whisper the message to the person on the right, and so on as children pass the message around the circle. Have the last person repeat the message aloud. After several rounds, ask:

▶ **Were our messages always heard correctly? Why or why not?**

▶ **What happened when you didn't hear the message?**

▶ **Do you think God always hears us? How do you know?**

Say: **Our thoughts, comments, messages, and prayers are very important to God—and he hears every one of them. In fact, the Bible tells us that God knows our thoughts before we even think them or say them! Isn't that neat? That shows how much God loves us. Let's see what else the Bible says about how God hears us.** Ask several volunteers to read aloud Psalm 4:3; Micah 7:7; and Psalm 34:15. Then ask:

▶ **What kinds of things can we tell God?**

▶ **Why is it nice to know that God always hears us?**

Say: **In our game of Telephone, we didn't always hear the message on the first or even second tries. It's good to know that we can trust God to hear us the first time—all the time! We can make a neat phone game to help younger kids learn that God always hears us.**

GET CRAFTIN'...

Spread newspapers around the floor and place the sections of hose in the center of the newspapers. Have children form the same number of small groups as you have hose sections. Give each group a section of hose and two plastic cups. Tell children that they'll be making Telephoses—funky hoses they can speak and listen through. Help children push the plastic cups over the ends of their sections of hose and then tightly secure the cups to the hose ends with duct tape. These will be the "receivers" and "speakers." Then invite children to decorate the hose sections by painting them with bright acrylic paints. Point out that the paints will dry faster if they're not spread on thickly. When one side of the hoses are painted, have children gently blow on the paint to speed drying time. Then carefully turn the hoses over and paint the other sides.

While the Telephoses dry, play several games of Telephone. Challenge kids to think up and whisper messages such as "God hears you when you pray," "We can talk to God any time," and "I'm glad that God always hears us." When the Telephoses are dry, let pairs take turns whispering into one end of the hose and listening in the cup at the opposite end. Challenge children to see how quietly they can whisper and still be heard. Remind kids that God hears us no matter how small our whispers are. Donate the colorful Telephoses to a class of younger children or toddlers and show them how to use the special phones. Be sure to have your children explain that God hears us whenever we talk and no matter how quietly we whisper.

Crafty Tips

▶ Use the Telephoses as start and finish lines for outdoor games.

Crafty Tips

▶ Place the Telephoses on the floor in any pattern. Challenge children to take a walk on make-believe "tightropes."

Hands, Toes, Feet, & Nose

So in Christ we who are many form one body, and each member belongs to all the others. Romans 12:5

Bible Craft Concept
We all have important parts to play in church.

Crafty Components
You'll need a Bible, craft glue, clear packing tape, pencils, crayons, newspaper, scissors, two medium-sized square boxes, and the following colors of construction paper: red, blue, yellow, and green. You'll also need photocopies of the patterns on page 52.

GET READY...

Before class, enlarge and photocopy onto stiff paper the body part illustrations on page 52. You'll need one each of the nose, knees, elbow, and ear. You'll need two each of the foot and hand. Cut out a foot and a hand to use as patterns. Set out the craft materials.

GET SET...

Gather children around the craft materials. Hold up paper body parts and ask kids to identify each. Then place the paper body parts on the floor and say: **Let's play a crazy game of What's Missing? Close your eyes, and I'll tap someone to sneak forward and snatch a paper body part. Then you can open your eyes and try to guess which picture is missing. When you think you know, hold up or point to that body part.** Play the game several times, then ask:

▶ **How do different parts of our bodies work together to help us function?**

▶ **What would happen if all the parts of our bodies did the same job?**

Say: **Just as the different parts of our bodies help us function, live, and work for God, the different people in our church help the church function, come to life, and work for God. And just as toes have a different job than fingers, different people in our church do different things. Some people are teachers,** some are good at singing, and others are wonderful at encouraging and cheering us. **What are other roles people play at our church?** Allow time for children to share their ideas. Then have a volunteer read aloud Romans 12:4-8 and 1 Corinthians 12:27-31. Ask:

▶ **Why do you think God gives us different gifts and talents to use in our church?**

▶ **What is one way you can help at church?**

Say: **It's good to remember that everyone in church plays an equally important role. We need each other just as the heart needs the brain. Let's make a great game to remind us how important it is that everyone has a special place in our church.**

Crafty Tips
▶ Use the playing cubes to identify rainbow colors in the story of Noah's ark.

GET CRAFTIN'...

Form three groups: the Color-Cubes, the Body-Boxers, and the Standers-n-Handers. Hand the Color-Cubes and Body-Boxers each a box. Have them stuff their boxes with crumpled newspapers to make them sturdier and then tape the boxes closed. Instruct the Color-Cubes to cover four sides of their box with red, yellow, blue, and green construction paper and to put stripes of each color on the two remaining sides. Have the Body-Boxers color and cut out the hand, nose, ear, foot, knees, and elbow shapes and glue one to each of the six sides of their box. Have the Standers-n-Handers use the foot and hand patterns to trace and cut out two each of the following colors: red, blue, green, and yellow. These shapes will be used as "bases" in the game.

Crafty Tips
▶ Invite grown-ups to play this giggly game with kids at your next church picnic. Have adults kneel on the bases.

To play, select two Rollers to roll the playing cubes. Then hand each remaining player a hand or foot base to stand on. (If there are more than ten children in your class, cut out extra bases or have children play in pairs.) Be sure the bases are grouped closely. Roll the playing cubes. If the cubes land on "red-nose," have the players standing on red bases put one finger on the nose of someone standing near them. If the cubes land on "striped-ear," have everyone put a finger on the ear of someone standing nearby. Continue rolling and playing until everyone is in a crazy tangle—or giggling too much to continue! Donate this fun game to a younger children's classroom and be sure to explain that just as different parts of the body work together, the people in your church work together in different ways.

Patterns for
Hands, Toes, Feet, & Nose

Enlarge and photocopy these patterns. You'll need one each of the nose, ear, elbow, and knees. You'll need two each of the foot and hand.

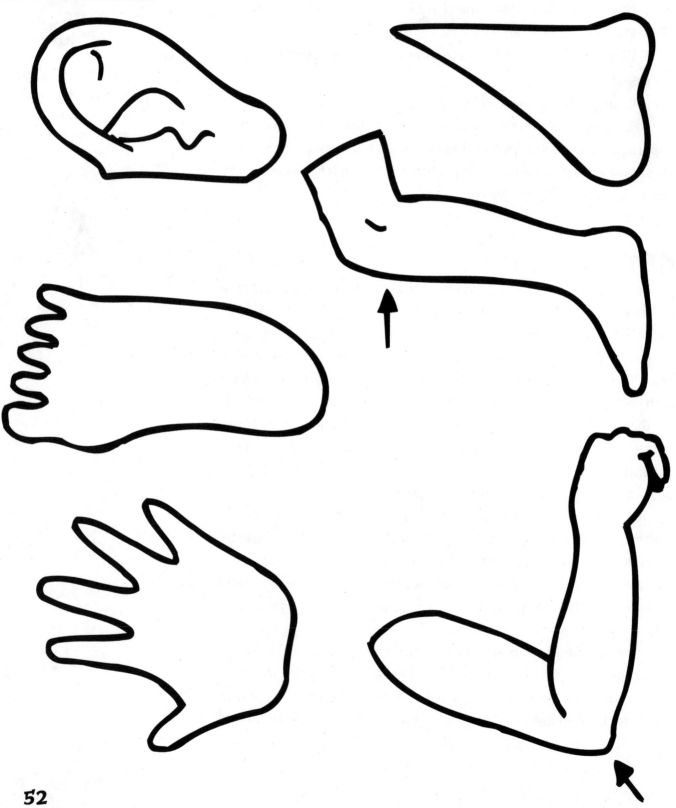

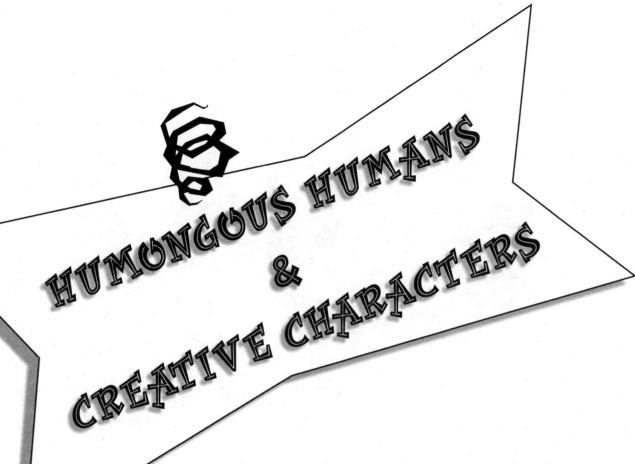

Chapter 3

HUMONGOUS HUMANS & CREATIVE CHARACTERS

Ponderous puppets, super-sized storytellers, immense Bible characters, jumbo Hug Me-Hold Me's—and lots more giant-sized fun!

One to Wear, One to Share

Live a life of love, just as Christ loved us. Ephesians 5:2

Bible Craft Concept
Jesus loves us.

Crafty Components
You'll need a Bible, tacky craft glue, self-adhesive Velcro dots, scissors, poster board, two 12" felt squares for each child, and extra felt for paws and facial features. You'll also need one or two yards of 36"-wide fake fur.

Velcro squares

GET READY...

Before class, cut the fake fur into 2"-by-36" strips. You'll need two strips for each child. Make a "Hug Me-Hold Me" to wear to class. (See the directions on page 55.)

GET SET...

Wear your Hug Me-Hold Me and gather children in small groups. Challenge each group to pantomime one way we show love or caring to someone. If a group is stuck for ideas, suggest hugs, pats on the back, smiles, or blowing kisses. Then have groups act out their ideas. When every group has acted out an idea, ask:

▶ **Why is demonstrating our love and caring important?**

▶ **How does Jesus show us his love? his care?**

▶ **Who can we show our love to?**

Say: **Jesus demonstrates his love for us in many ways. The Bible tells us the most loving way was dying for our sins. Jesus also shows us love by helping us, by teaching us about God's truths, and by sending us the Holy Spirit. Let's read what else the Bible tells us about Jesus' love and who we can love.** Ask a volunteer to read aloud Ephesians 5:1-2. Then say: **Jesus loves us so much. I can almost feel his warm hug around me, can't you? Mmm—see how my Hug Me-Hold Me gives me a warm, loving hug?**

We can show how much Jesus loves us by making cool Hug Me-Hold Me's to wear. In fact, let's make one Hug Me-Hold Me to wear—and one to share. That way we can spread Jesus' love to others!

GET CRAFTIN'...

Hand each child two squares of felt, two strips of fake fur, and two sets of sticky Velcro dots. Explain that a Hug Me-Hold Me is a giant "hug" to wear around a person's neck and shoulders.

To make a Hug Me-Hold Me, cut out a large circle "head" from one square of felt. Use the felt as a pattern to cut a matching head from poster board. Glue the felt head to the poster board head for extra support. Then glue the back of the felt head to the fuzzy side of one strip of fake fur, centering the head along the strip to create two long "arms." Cut out two felt "paws" or "hands" from the felt and glue them to the fuzzy ends of the fake fur. Cut out felt facial features and short floppy ears, then glue them to the head. Separate one set of Velcro dots and stick one dot on the "palm" of each paw or hand. Then set the first Hug Me-Hold Me aside while you construct a second one.

When you're finished, wrap a Hug Me-Hold Me around your neck and shoulders, then fasten the paws together to make a warm "hug." Let each child wear one Hug Me-Hold Me home and decide who he or she would like to give the "one to share" to. Suggest elderly church members, kids at a children's hospital, or missionary kids.

Crafty Tips
▶ Have older children write a note to attach to their Hug Me-Hold Me's. Suggest a note or poem telling about Jesus' love.

Crafty Tips
▶ For a clever fund-raiser, have kids make a colorful crowd of Hug Me-Hold Me's. Display them on hangers and sell your "hugs" for $5.00 plus a **real** hug! Donate proceeds to a center for homeless children or adults.

Giant Puppet Pals

For it is by grace you have been saved, through faith. Ephesians 2:8

Bible Craft Concept
God wants us to have faith in him.

Crafty Components
You'll need a Bible, five large sheets of poster board, markers, glue, scissors, colored construction paper, and a variety of tactile embellishments such as fabric, aluminum foil, shiny wrapping paper, cotton balls, sandpaper, glitter glue, yarn, and sequins. Optional: duct tape and ½"-by-4' dowel rods.

GET READY...

Place the craft materials on the floor.

GET SET...

Gather children into small groups. Say: **Let's do something different. Within your group, brainstorm a nursery rhyme character to act out. Some characters might include Little Bo-Peep, the mouse in Hickory Dickory Dock, or Little Miss Muffet. In a few moments, each group will have a turn to act out its characters to see if others can guess who they're imitating.** After all the groups have acted out their characters, ask:

▶ **What are the differences between make-believe people and things and real people and things?**

▶ **Which are easier to trust? Why?**

▶ **How can we show we have real faith in God—not just make-believe faith?**

Say: **Make-believe faith is trusting in make-believe gods such as money or sports heroes. Make-believe faith isn't faith at all. It is based on nothing and does nothing to help us. Solid faith comes from knowing, loving, and following the one, true God—and this faith helps us all the time! How do we know what real faith is? Let's look in the Bible.** Have several volunteers read aloud Hebrews 11:1; James 2:22; and Ephesians 2:8, 9. Then ask:

▶ **In what ways does our faith in God help us each day?**

▶ **How can we develop deeper faith in God?**

Say: **In the Bible, people such as Moses, Joshua, Mary, Ruth, and Jesus' disciples had faith in God. And just like these Bible people, we can have faith in God, too! We can know, love, and follow God each day. Let's make giant puppets of some of the Bible characters who had giant faith in God. These puppets will help us tell Bible stories and also remind us that God wants us to have faith in him!**

Crafty Tips
▶ Use these humongous puppets to tell the following stories: Ruth and Naomi, the Good Samaritan, the birth of Jesus, and Noah!

GET CRAFTIN'...

Form five groups. Let each group choose one of the following pairs of characters: young woman/old woman, young man/old man, good king/mean king, boy/girl, and donkey/sheep. Explain that these huge puppets will be reversible because they'll have faces on both sides. Have each group cut a huge head from poster board and then decide how to draw, color, and embellish its two-sided character. For example, the kings could wear shiny crowns with paper jewels, but the good king might smile and the mean king sport a growly scowl. The women could wear fabric headbands, while the puppet children might have yarn hair. Sandpaper would work well for the men's wooden staffs, and cotton balls would embellish the sheep nicely. As children work, encourage them to think of Bible stories that illustrate faith, stories such as Noah and the ark or Peter in prison.

When the puppets are finished, let kids admire the characters and think of real Bible characters they could represent. Finished puppets can be held high or taped to stout dowel rods for "puppets-on-a-stick." If there's time, let children use the puppets to tell a Bible story. Donate the huge characters to the church for skits or decorations, to younger classes for storytelling tools, or to your VBS program.

Crafty Tips
▶ Make an instant puppet stage by draping a solid color sheet over a long table. Have kids hold the puppet heads above the table as they hide from the audience.

The Very Large Looking Glass

The Lord looks at the heart. 1 Samuel 16:7

Bible Craft Concept
God looks at our hearts.

Crafty Components
You'll need a Bible, several rolls of colored electrical tape, markers, poster board, scissors, clear packing tape, and an inexpensive full-length mirror. Be sure the mirror is framed.

GET READY...

Purchase a framed full-length mirror from a discount store—or check garage sales, flea markets, or church members' attics for next-to-nothing full-length mirrors.

GET SET...

Have children form pairs. Instruct partners to face each other and then take turns describing what they see. Be sure to let someone describe you, too! Then ask:

▶ **What do most people look at when they see someone?**

▶ **Why do you think people look at how others dress, how tall they are, or the color of their hair?**

▶ **How do you think God looks at us?**

Say: **When we look at someone or even at ourselves in a mirror, we see only what's on the outside. But God sees us differently. God looks at our hearts and the way we are on the inside. Let's read what the Bible tells us about the way God sees us.** Ask a volunteer to read aloud 1 Samuel 16:7. Then ask:

▶ **How does looking at the "inside" of someone give a better picture of that person?**

▶ Why do you think God is more concerned with how we think and feel than with how we look?

▶ How does knowing God sees you this way affect your behavior? how you treat others?

Say: **God looks at the inside of our hearts—not at our outward appearances. Each time you look in a mirror, you can remember that people see the outside but that God sees the inside! Let's decorate a wonderful mirror to give to others so they can learn how God looks at people, too.**

GET CRAFTIN'...

Lay the mirror on the floor, reflective side up. Let children use the colorful tape to make snazzy decorations and colorful designs around the edges of the mirror, directly on the glass surface. Then make and decorate four question cards to tape along the mirror's edges. Use questions such as "What does God see?" "Who does God love?" "Who is Jesus' friend?" and "Whose heart loves Jesus?" Use rolled tape to attach the cards to the edges of the decorated mirror. As children work, talk about the way God sees us. Point out that God doesn't need a mirror to see who we are because God looks at our hearts instead.

When the mirror is done, donate your beautiful creation to a younger children's classroom (to be used with adult supervision) or to the church for use in a restroom. You may even wish to present this special mirror as a gift to the pastor to place behind his or her office door.

Crafty Tips
▶ Get permission for your children to use colored tape to decorate the wall mirrors in the church restrooms. Encourage children to use geometric designs and rainbow colors to spruce up the mirrors and add a cheery touch to often dull rooms!

Crafty Tips
▶ Older children might enjoy painting the edges of mirrors with bright acrylic paints or paints for stained glass. Check local craft stores for a super selection of paints!

Super Shepherd and Sheep

I am the good shepherd. John 10:14

Bible Craft Concept
Jesus is our good shepherd.

Crafty Components
You'll need a Bible, a yard of fabric, poster board, crayons, markers, glue, scissors, rope, clear packing tape, paper grocery sacks, cotton balls, white garbage bags, newspapers, rubber bands or twist-tie wires, and construction paper. You'll also need a 36"-tall round tomato cage.

GET READY...

Obtain a tomato cage from a discount garden shop or a church member who gardens. Place the craft materials on the floor.

GET SET...

Gather children and ask:

▶ **What does a shepherd do?**

▶ **How does a shepherd care for his sheep?**

▶ **How do you know if a shepherd is doing a good job caring for his sheep?**

Say: **Did you know that Jesus tells us he is a good shepherd and we are his sheep? What do you think Jesus means?** Allow children to express their ideas. Then say: **Just as a good shepherd protects his flock and provides for their needs, Jesus protects us and provides for our needs.** Ask:

▶ **How does Jesus keep us safe? supply our needs?**

▶ **Can we trust Jesus as sheep trust their shepherd? Explain.**

Say: **Let's read what the Bible says about Jesus being the good shepherd.** Ask several volunteers to read aloud Psalm 23:1 and John 10:14-16. Then say: **I'm so glad our shepherd is Jesus! Let's make a good**

shepherd and his fluffy sheep to remind us that Jesus is the perfect good shepherd in our lives.

GET CRAFTIN'...

Form three groups: one to make the shepherd and two to make the sheep. For the shepherd's head, cut a large circle of poster board and color it light brown. Add eyes and a nose and a cotton ball beard. Stretch the cotton balls for a more realistic effect. Set the tomato cage upright on the floor, then tape the paper head to the top of the tomato cage. Drape fabric around the cage to create a "robe," then tape the robe in place. Tie rope or cord around the "waist" for a belt. Cut out construction paper "shoes" and tape them under the robe so they peek out. Glue rope and fabric around the shepherd's forehead for a "headpiece." Twist-fold paper grocery sacks to make a "staff" and tape it to the shepherd's side.

To make the sheep, stuff white garbage bags with newspaper. Use rubber bands or twist-tie wires to seal the bags and make the sheep's "tails." Use a black marker to draw a face on the sheep. Cut ears from black construction paper and tape them to the sides of the face. Glue cotton balls to the sheep for "lamb's wool."

Use the shepherd and sheep as storytelling props, as skit scenery, or as three-dimensional church displays to remind people that Jesus is the good shepherd and that we are his sheep.

Colossal Caterpillar Pushees

If anyone is in Christ, he is a new creation. 2 Corinthians 5:17

Bible Craft Concept
Jesus gives us new life.

Crafty Components
You'll need a Bible, 19-gauge steel wire, scissors, tacky craft glue, construction paper, chenille wires, and a 2' section of feather boa for each child, plus a few extras.

GET READY...

Cut the wire into 1'-long pieces. Cut two pieces for each child. Feather boas and wire can be purchased at most craft stores. Make a "Pushee" to use as children arrive.

GET SET...

Make Mr. Caterpillar (the Pushee) wriggle and twist when it "sees" the children. Have Mr. Caterpillar say: **Wow! Look at all the caterpillars! But they're not very fuzzy!** Teacher: **That's because they're not caterpillars—they're children. You're the only fuzzy caterpillar here.** Mr. Caterpillar: **Not for long! I'm gonna wiggle n' wriggle n' spin a cocoon—and do you know what I'll be when I come out? A butterfly! Nothin's better than being a butterfly! It's like I'll have a whole new life! I'll bet YOU can't do that!** Teacher: **Well, Mr. Caterpillar, that's not true. We all can have new lives because someone very special died to give us new life. Kids, can you tell Mr. Caterpillar who can give us new life?** Allow kids to respond. Then have Mr. Caterpillar say: **Jesus died to give you new life? But how does that make you new?** Encourage children to explain how Jesus forgives us and helps us live and love as God's friends. Then say: **Let's read Mr. Caterpillar something from the Bible.** Have several children read aloud 2 Corinthians 5:17. Then make Mr. Caterpillar squiggle and wiggle with glee. Mr. Caterpillar: **Wowie! You sure can have new** life—and it's even better than being a butterfly!

Set the Pushee aside and say: **Let's celebrate the joy of new life with Jesus by making fuzzy Pushee caterpillars. They'll remind us that just as caterpillars have new life as butterflies, we can have new life as God's friends!**

GET CRAFTIN'...

Hand each child a section of feather boa and two pieces of wire. Explain that kids will be making fuzzy caterpillar puppets called Pushees. For each Pushee, twist a loop of wire around each end of the feather boa. Tear or cut out construction paper features such as eyes, noses, or smiles, then glue them to one end, between the wire and the end of the boa. Add chenille wire "antennas" by twisting the wires around the boa. Make several extra Pushees to donate to another class for impromptu skits and lessons.

When the Pushees are finished, let children practice pushing the wires up and down and watching their adorable Pushees wriggle, wiggle, twist, and twirl. Then invite children to form pairs and to brainstorm a short skit using their caterpillar Pushees. Challenge kids to focus their skits on some aspect of new life in Jesus, such as forgiveness, loving others, giving thanks, or the importance of prayer. Have kids present the skits to each other and then show them to another class. Have your class give the extra Pushees you made to the other class, then challenge the other children to create skits about Jesus' love.

Crafty Tips
▶ Make stuffed paper apples from painted grocery sacks. Cut a large hole in the center of each sack and stuff the Pushee inside. It's so cute when Pushees creep out!

Crafty Tips
▶ Present a colorful Pushee to the children's worship leader, if your church has one. Or gift wrap the Pushee and present it to the children's minister, a sick child, or someone who needs a special smile.

Hands to Serve

It is the Lord Christ you are serving. Colossians 3:24

Bible Craft Concept
We can serve Jesus in many ways.

Crafty Components
You'll need a Bible, several rolls of aluminum foil, transparent tape, scissors, clear packing tape, fishing line, and several 3' to 4' sections of ¼" dowel rod.

GET READY...

Place the craft materials on the floor.

GET SET...

This very unique craft idea works best with older children—or with older and younger children paired. Gather children and ask:

▶ **What does it mean to "serve" someone?**

▶ **When is a time someone served you? In what way were you served?**

▶ **Why do you think serving others is good?**

Say: **Serving others is very important. In fact, Jesus spent a lot of time teaching us to be good servants. Jesus even said that he was among people to serve them.** Read aloud Mark 10:45 and Colossians 3:23, 24. Then say: **Jesus showed us what servanthood is all about when he washed the feet of his disciples at the last supper. Jesus demonstrated how important it is for each of us to serve others with love and kindness. In what ways can we serve others?** Lead children to name ways such as caring for someone who's ill, telling another person about Jesus, cheering up someone who's had a rough day, and donating our time, talents, or money to help people. Then say: **When our hands and hearts serve others, we're really** serving Jesus. Jesus told us that when we do something for someone else, we're doing it for him, too. Let's make a super-shiny mobile to remind everyone that serving others with hearts and hands means serving Jesus, too!

GET CRAFTIN'...

Have children form pairs or trios. Hand each child two 2'-long pieces of aluminum foil. Explain that kids are going to use aluminum foil to make molds of their hands. Show children how one partner can lay his or her hand on the floor, fingers spread, so the other partner can place a piece of foil over the hand and carefully push the foil around each finger. Tell children to mold the entire hand one finger at a time. After the back of the hand is covered with foil, gently lift the foil from the hand and use scissors to carefully trim around the edges. Have kids make molds of both their hands.

Cut varying lengths of fishing line and tape the pieces of line to the aluminum hand molds at various places, such as at the wrist, the thumb, or one of the fingers. Use packing tape, fishing line, and dowel rods to construct a simple mobile frame. Suspend the shiny hands from the ends of the dowels rods. Make several aluminum foil heart shapes by twisting long pieces of foil. Add the shiny hearts to your mobile.

Donate your unique creation to the church as an appealing ceiling display for the sanctuary or for a vaulted entryway. For a special touch, add a sign that reads: "Many hands to serve…Many hearts to love."

Crafty Tips

▶ Set up a table with foil, scissors, tape, and fishing line. Have kids invite adults to make molds of their hands, then add them to the display. Have children serve the adults by offering help and giving instructions.

Crafty Tips

▶ Use this idea for a fun fund-raiser. Simply make a number of hand molds, then have church members write their names and pledge amounts on slips of paper to tape to the foil hands. Suspend the hands as they're collected.

Super Stuffies

I am fearfully and wonderfully made. Psalm 139:14

Bible Craft Concept
God made each one of us special.

Crafty Components
You'll need a Bible, several rolls of white shelf paper, markers, tape, scissors, construction paper, a stapler, glue, and newspapers.

God's love made us special, that is true—God celebrates us, He celebrates you!

GET READY...

Place the craft items on the floor. Cut the white shelf paper into 5' lengths. You'll need two lengths of shelf paper for each child in class.

GET SET...

Have children form small groups. Challenge each group to decide how its members are alike and different. Then encourage children to tell one or two things about themselves that makes them special or unique. Kids might name a hobby they have or something they're really good at in school. After several minutes of sharing, gather children in a large group. Invite group members to introduce each other by saying, "This is (name) and he (or she) is special because (fill in the blank)." After each person has been introduced, lead the class in a lively round of applause. When all the children have been introduced, ask:

▶ **What makes each of us special?**

▶ **Is everyone special in some way? Explain.**

Say: **Each person is precious to God, and that's why he made us so special. God gave different gifts and talents to each of us, too. Let's read what the Bible says about how God made us special.** Read aloud Psalm 139:13-16. Then say: **Sometimes we forget how special we are to God. But God doesn't make junk—**

66

and we're special because God loves us! Let's make giant "Stuffies" to remind us how special we are to God.

GET CRAFTIN'...

Let children work in pairs or trios. Have each person lie down on a piece of shelf paper while partners trace around the outline of his or her body. Tape another piece of shelf paper behind the tracing, then cut out the two outlines. Staple the edges of the outlines half way around, then stuff the figure with slightly crumpled newspapers. Continue stapling and stuffing until the figure is slightly plump and three dimensional. Invite children to color their Stuffies any way they choose. For a colorful touch, add construction paper facial features, hair, or clothing. To make curly hair, simply roll strips of colored paper around a marker. Tell children to add features that make them special, such as freckles, dimples, or that "always there" skinned knee!

When the Stuffies are complete, hold them up and let children try to guess who they represent. Then arrange the Stuffies down a long hallway with the following sign: "God's love made us special, that is true. God celebrates us, and he celebrates YOU!"

Crafty Tips
▶ Stuffies are great fun for parents visiting your classroom. Have children write and tape to their Stuffies note cards that tell reasons they're special.

Crafty Tips
▶ Stuffies make great background "crowds" for kids' skits—and these extras don't need bathroom breaks!
▶ For a fun variation, let children make "Bible Stuffies" of their favorite biblical characters.

Praise Angels

I will extol the Lord with all my heart. Psalm 111:1

Bible Craft Concept
We can praise the Lord.

Crafty Components
You'll need a Bible, a dishpan, newspapers, two bottles of fabric stiffener, glitter, balloons, metallic chenille wires, three plastic wastebaskets, glue, and three yards of lightweight white cotton or cheesecloth.

GET READY...
Be sure all three fabric pieces are at least 36" square.

GET SET...
Have kids form small groups and read Psalm 148:1-14. Then say: **This psalm from the Bible is called a praise psalm. It praises God in a beautiful poem for who he is and for all he has made and done.** Ask:

▶ **What does it mean to praise God?**

▶ **How does praise show God our love?**

▶ **Why is it important to praise God?**

Say: **Praising God is a good way to tell God we love him and to show others we love God, too. Listen while I read how David praised God.** Read aloud Psalm 103:1-4.

Then say: **People aren't the only ones who can praise God. Listen to this story. When you know who's being praised, raise one hand. When you know who's giving praise, raise your other hand.** Read aloud Luke 2:8-14. When children's hands are up, ask them who was giving praise and who the angels were praising. Then ask:

▶ **Why did the angels praise God?**

▶ **How did the angels praise and announce Jesus' birth?**

▶ **In what ways can we show our praises?**

Say: **We can praise the Lord in many ways—through songs, prayers, poems, and by the way we live our lives. Let's show our praise by making reminders of the first ones to praise God for the arrival of Jesus—the angels!**

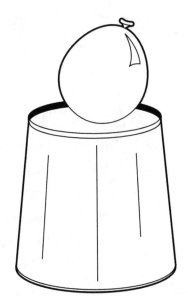

GET CRAFTIN'...

Spread newspapers on the floor. (If you have carpeting, you may want to spread an old shower curtain under the papers.) Place the dishpan on the papers and fill it with fabric stiffener. Form three groups and hand each group a wastebasket, a balloon, and a yard of fabric. Instruct groups to blow up their balloons and set them on top of their overturned wastebaskets. Have children dip their fabric in the fabric stiffener and squeeze out excess liquid. Then have kids drape and arrange the fabric over the balloon and wastebasket, pinching the fabric to make "arms." Sprinkle glitter over the "body" portion of the angel. Bend metallic chenille wires into "halos" and glue them to the "heads." Set the angels aside to dry. When they are dry, pop the balloons and remove the wastebaskets. If you would like, embellish the angels with lace, ribbon, or "angel hair."

Present the praise angels to the minister or worship leader as decorations for the congregation to enjoy. These sparkly heralds may be placed in the worship area, set beside bright poinsettias, or suspended from tall ceilings with wire or fishing line.

Crafty Tips

▶ Shiny Christmas tree ornaments of trumpets and harps can be glued to the angels for a lovely effect.

▶ Use permanent markers to add eyes and "singing" mouths to the angels when they're dry. Add paper doilies for wings.

A Whale of a Fish!

father, I thank you that you have heard me. John 11:41

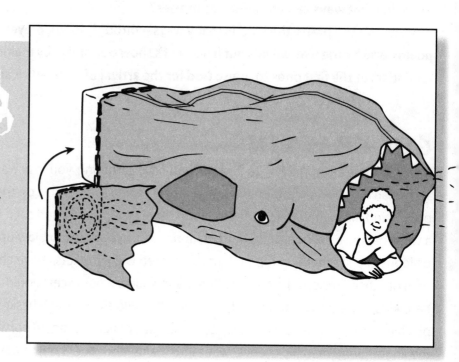

Bible Craft Concept
God answers prayer.

Crafty Components
You'll need a Bible, duct tape, two large rolls of black plastic, a box floor fan, construction paper, scissors, clear tape, and markers.

GET READY...

Make sure the rolls of plastic are approximately 10'-by-25' or whichever roll size is nearest to these dimensions.

GET SET...

Gather children in a group and ask:

▶ **When is a time you asked for something and received it?**

▶ **Do you always get what you ask for? Why or why not?**

▶ **How is prayer an example of asking for what we need?**

▶ **Does God always answer our prayers or give us what we ask for? Explain.**

Say: **Because God loves us, he always answers our prayers. God answers our prayers in his time and in the way he thinks is best. Sometimes that doesn't fit the way we want God to answer. But we can trust God to answer our prayers in the way that's best for us. Let's read what the Bible says about God answering our prayers.** Have several children read aloud John 11:41, 42; Psalm 34:17; and Jonah 2:1. Then say: **When Jonah was swallowed by the big fish, he was afraid. So Jonah prayed. For three days and nights, Jonah sat in the tummy of that big fish and prayed. Did God hear and answer his prayers?** Allow children to recount the story and how God answered Jonah's prayers by having the fish spit Jonah on the sand.

Then say: **Jonah was very thankful that God heard and answered his prayers—and we're thankful that God answers our prayers, too! Let's make a whale of a big fish to help other kids learn how Jonah found out that God answers prayers.**

Crafty Tips

▶ Use this same technique to create a "cave" to help tell the story of the first Easter morning or of Jesus' birth in the stable/cave.

GET CRAFTIN'...

Have children help spread the two rolls of black plastic side by side on the floor and then tape them together down the center. Have children hold the four corners and take four giant steps toward the center to reduce the width of the shorter sides by about one half. Then ask children to hold the plastic ends while you tape the long edges of the plastic to the floor. Place a large box fan at one end of the plastic so the breeze blows inward. Position the taped seam on the top center of the fan and tape it in place. Then tape the plastic around the fan and along the floor on both sides. On the opposite end, scoot the plastic inward about one foot, then have children tape that end to the floor. Cut a 5' opening on top of the plastic as shown in the illustration on page 70. Turn the fan on high to inflate the huge "fish"; then set the fan on a lower setting. Invite children to embellish their fishy creation with paper teeth, construction paper eyes, and colorful paper "fins."

When the fish is complete, invite everyone to sit inside and hear the story of Jonah from a colorful picture book. End your time with a prayer thanking God for hearing and answering our prayers. Then have your class invite another class to sit inside your fishy creation as they hear the story of Jonah. Be sure to encourage your children to explain that God hears and answers prayers—in his time and in his way.

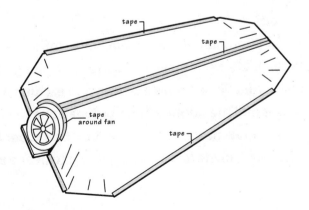

Giant Bible Storyteller

Your word is a lamp to my feet and a light for my path. Psalm 119:105

Bible Craft Concept
We can learn about God from the Bible.

Crafty Components
You'll need a Bible, fiberfill, tacky craft glue, construction paper, rope, markers, scissors, a bell, several inexpensive short Bible-story picture books, and a cassette recorder and blank tape. You'll also need a large paper barrel or large tall box.

GET READY...

Ask a hardware store to donate a large cardboard nail barrel for this activity. Or purchase a tall packing box from a moving company. Cut arm holes and facial openings in the barrel or box according to the illustration.

GET SET...

Hold up the Bible and ask:

▶ **What's included in the Bible?**

▶ **What are some of your favorite Bible stories?**

▶ **How does the Bible help us learn about God?**

Say: **The Bible teaches us so many wonderful things about God. From Bible stories, we learn how important it is to pray, to obey, and to have faith. Bible stories teach us God's truth and give good examples for living the way God wants us to live. And Bible stories are a fun and exciting way to learn about God! Just think of Noah and the ark, Moses and the burning bush, or Jonah and the huge fish. Learning about God through Bible stories helps us draw nearer to God. Let's make a super Bible story-teller to tell exciting stories from the Bible. Then we'll invite lots of other people to hear a Bible story and learn more about God!**

GET CRAFTIN'...

Show children the illustration of this project and explain that they'll be turning the giant box or barrel into a Bible character who "tells" stories. Then form two groups: Builders and Recorders. Builders will build the Bible character, while Recorders will tape-record Bible stories from the book or books you've chosen. Have the Recorders go to a quiet area to record the stories. Tell them to ring the bell after reading each page. This will clue in page-turners later on. Have the Builders embellish the barrel or box to look like Moses or Noah. Use fiberfill for hair and a beard, construction paper for shoes and a robe, and rope for a belt.

When the recordings and the Bible character are complete, ask a volunteer page-turner to stand inside the box and place his or her arms through the arm holes. Have the page-turner hold a storybook and turn the pages after each bell sound. Gather everyone in front of the storyteller character and start the recording. When the story is over, donate the storyteller character, books, and tape to a younger children's classroom or the children's church director. Be sure to offer your children's services for the "inside" job of page-turners!

Crafty Tips
▶ Use this super storytelling technique with VBS, Sunday school—or any time you want a fun Bible story presentation or instant story costume.

Crafty Tips
▶ Consider inviting parents to join in listening to the Bible stories. Serve refreshments and turn your gathering into a Bible story party!

Chapter 4

COLOSSAL CLASSROOMS & DYNAMITE DISPLAYS

Colossal classroom resources, sensational scenery, enormous banners and flags, giant fantasy flowers, and dynamite whole-church displays!

A Big Banner of BIG Love

We love because God first loved us. 1 John 4:19 (ICB)

Bible Craft Concept
God's love for us is huge!

Crafty Components
You'll need a Bible, felt squares, tacky craft glue, scissors, braid, stapler, black permanent marker, and a 3'-by-5' piece of yellow felt. You'll also need a few smooth stones and various craft scraps such as buttons, yarn, ribbons, lace, and sequins. You may wish to use pre-cut paper or fabric letters instead of a black marker.

GET READY...

Set out the craft items and spread the large piece of felt on the floor. Arrange with the pastor to allow children to present their banner to the congregation at the end of the church service.

GET SET...

Gather children in a circle and have them take one minute to look at everyone present. Then tell children to cover their eyes. Ask:

▶ **Who are the people you saw in our circle?**

▶ **How are all the people in our room alike? different?**

▶ **What am I wearing? What color are my eyes? How tall do you think I am?**

Have children uncover their eyes. Say: **You noticed a lot about the people in our room, but you probably didn't notice many of the "little things" such as what color someone is wearing or how tall he or she is. But there's someone who knows everything about us—even down to exactly how tall each of us is. Do you know who that is?** Let children tell their ideas. Then say: **God knows everything about each one of us. God knows when we're happy or sad, how old we are, what we're thinking, and even how many hairs are on each of our heads! Let's read what the Bible says about how much God knows about us.**

Ask several volunteers to read aloud each verse of Psalm 139:1-6. Say: **God loves us and knows so much about us because he made us. God's love is wonderful!** Then ask:

▶ **Is there any one of God's children whom he doesn't love? Explain.**

▶ **Why is it important to let others know how much God loves them?**

Say: **God's love is so big that it covers every one of his children. That means that God loves us all equally. Isn't that great? It's so great, let's tell everyone in our church how big God's love is by making a big, big, BIG picture to hang on the wall. That way everyone will remember that God loves each one of us!**

GET CRAFTIN'...

Let children work in pairs to make fun "felt faces." Give each child a colorful felt square to create a large circle, square, triangle, or heart shape. Make sure the shapes are at least 6" wide or long. Then invite children to use buttons, scrap felt, ribbons, sequins, braid, and other craft materials to decorate the felt "faces." As children work, lay the smooth stones in a row about 3" above the bottom edge of the large felt piece. Staple the stones in the "hem" of your banner. Then glue a length of braid over the staples.

When the felt faces are finished, position them around the bottom half to third of the banner. Then have children use tacky craft glue to attach the faces. To finish the banner, let children use the black permanent marker to write the following rhyme in large letters across the top portion of the banner. (For a "neater" look, let kids glue on pre-cut bulletin board or iron-on letters.)

No matter what size or shape or name,
God loves his people all the same!

After the banner is finished, invite children to carry their labor of love into the church to present to the congregation. Ask several adults if they'd be willing to hang the banner high on a wall for everyone to enjoy. As children leave, have them each hug several people and say, "God loves you!"

Crafty Tips
▶ To display this banner on a wall, staple a "hem" along the top edge of the felt, then slip a wooden dowel into the hem pocket. Tie cord to the ends of the dowel for a hanger.

Crafty Tips
▶ Let kids make "mini-banners" from small squares of felt and paper heart shapes. Encourage children to hang their banners in their homes to remind their families of God's abiding love.

Confetti Lights

I have come into the world as a light. *John 12:46*

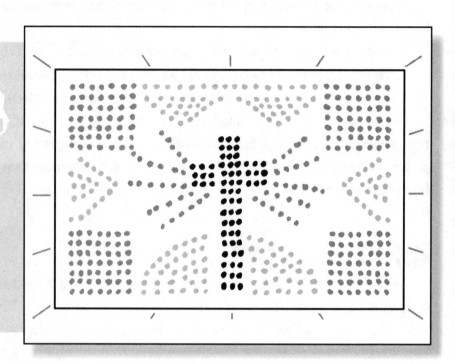

Bible Craft Concept
Jesus is the light of the world.

Crafty Components
You'll need a Bible, opaque stained glass paint or pastel acrylic paints, paintbrushes, newspapers, and one or two fluorescent light panels.

GET READY...

Purchase fluorescent light panels from discount hardware stores or building supply centers. These are the clear bumpy panels that cover fluorescent ceiling lights.

GET SET...

Form pairs and challenge partners to think of things that give light or brightness to the world. Allow several minutes for partners to share thoughts, then have each pair join another pair and share their responses. Continue joining pairs until the entire class is one large group. Then ask:

▶ **Of all the lights you mentioned, which is brightest? What makes it so bright?**

▶ **What does light do for us?**

▶ **What would the world be like if there were no light and only darkness?**

Say: **Jesus called himself a light to the world. How is Jesus like a light to the world?**

Allow children to tell their ideas. Then say: **Let's see what the Bible says about Jesus being the light of the world.** Ask for several volunteers to read aloud John 12:44-46. Then ask:

▶ **How does Jesus' light keep us safe from the darkness of evil?**

▶ **In what ways does the bright light of Jesus help you see more clearly every day?**

Say: **Jesus' love and truth shine like a bright light to the world. And when we love Jesus, we live in that light and stay safe. Jesus' light is the brightest light the world has ever known! Let's make a colossal confetti window-light to remind everyone of the beautiful light Jesus brings into the world.**

GET CRAFTIN'...

Spread newspapers on the floor and lay the fluorescent panels on the paper. Have children form pairs and hand each pair two paintbrushes and a bottle of paint. Invite children to paint the bumps on the plastic in "confetti-fashion"—that is, randomly painting the bumps different colors around the panels. Every several minutes, encourage children to exchange paint colors and brushes with other pairs. Older children may wish to create a particular design for the center of the panels—such as a heart, a cross, or a dove—and then fill in the rest of the bumps confetti-style. As kids work, ask questions such as "How does Jesus' light help us steer clear of bad things?" and "How can we thank Jesus for being the light of the world?" Encourage children to mention ways to thank Jesus, such as prayer, helping spread Jesus' light to others, and keeping Jesus as the focus of their lives.

When the confetti panels are dry, help children choose a church window in which to set them. Then stand back and admire the sunny stained glass effect. End the activity with a quiet prayer thanking Jesus for being our light of love. If you can't find an appropriate window, donate the colorful confetti panels to the toddlers' room or nursery, where they can be placed over fluorescent light fixtures.

Crafty Tips
▶ For a fun twist, play lively music as children paint. Each time you stop the music or a song ends, have children trade paint colors and brushes.

Crafty Tips
▶ If your children enjoyed this activity, invite them to paint baby food jars with stained glass paint. When the jars are dry, glue chunky 2" candles to the jar lids. Group the candles on a table at the next church potluck for a "light-bright" centerpiece.

Wonderful Wallflower Garden

As the Father has loved me, so have I loved you. John 15:9

Bible Craft Concept
We can grow and spread God's love.

Crafty Components
You'll need a Bible, construction paper, colored tissue paper, duct tape, clear tape, scissors, paper grocery sacks, green crepe paper, colored disposable plastic bowls, and permanent markers.

GET READY...

Choose a wall for your children to embellish. Classrooms, hallways, or fellowship rooms make great places for this colossal garden of love.

GET SET...

Choose pairs of children to act out the following motions: planting seeds, watering a garden, picking weeds, hoeing a garden, and picking beautiful flowers. Let children guess what is being acted out, then ask:

▶ **Which is more important: planting seeds or caring for them? Explain.**

Say: **Seeds need water and warm sunshine to grow and spread. How can we make our love grow and spread to others?** Encourage children to mention doing kind things to others and reading the Bible to learn more about God's love. Then say: **Let's see what the Bible says about God's love and how we can spread love to others.**

Have children read aloud Matthew 22:37-39; John 15:9; and 1 John 4:11, 19. Then ask:

▶ **Why are we able to love others?**

▶ **What happens when we spread God's love to others?**

Say: **When we spread God's love to others, it's like planting a beautiful garden of love. The love grows** and spreads, and everyone enjoys the beauty. Let's make a giant garden on the wall to remind us to grow and spread God's love to everyone.

GET CRAFTIN'...

Look at the illustration to plan your garden together. Then form three groups: the Tree-Sowers, the Grass-Mowers, and the Flower-Growers. Tree-Sowers will construct two tremendous trees along the wall by twisting brown paper grocery sacks into "tree trunks." Use rolled duct tape to attach the trunks to the wall. Place three or four twisted sacks together for thick trunks, then add twisted sacks for tree branches. Trees should reach to within a few feet of the ceiling, so you may need tall adults to "donate their height." When the trunks are done, tear large green construction paper "leaves" to tape from the branches. Be sure lots of leaves swing out into the room and aren't just taped flat to the wall.

Grass-Mowers can cut or tear green construction paper into tall, fringed grass fronds and tape them to the wall. Have the Grass-Mowers begin in the center of the wall and work downward and outward, making layers of paper grass that reach to the floor. Use various shades of green for a 3-D effect. Have Flower-Growers tape colorful plastic bowls to the wall at different heights for flower-centers. Let children draw their faces on the bowls. Then tear out construction paper "petals" and tape them around the bowls for humongous daisies. Gather sheets of tissue paper into huge posies and tape them to twisted crepe paper "stems" on the wall. Finally, add twisted green crepe paper "vines" with torn paper leaves to your delightful display.

When you're finished, the entire wall should resemble a lush tropical garden! Have your children invite younger children to sit in front of the wall as your class explains that God loves us and that we're like his garden of love—we can bloom and spread God's love to everyone.

Crafty Tips
▶ If you can't find a wall to decorate, consider decorating "garden doors" for classrooms and restrooms.

Crafty Tips
▶ To dismantle your crafty display, invite children to pick flowers, grasses, vines, and leaves from the garden to take home. You'll be surprised how quickly the display will "disappear"!

The Christian Flag Banner

There is but one Lord, Jesus Christ. 1 Corinthians 8:6

Bible Craft Concept
We serve one Savior, Jesus Christ.

Crafty Components
You'll need a Bible, gold fringe, gold braid, pre-cut paper or fabric letters, tacky craft glue, a 4'-by-4' piece of purple fabric, a 2'-by-3' piece of white cotton, an 8" square of dark blue fabric, one square of red craft felt, and two 4'-by-¼" dowel rods.

GET READY...

Before class, stiffen the fabric pieces with fabric stiffener or heavy starch. Dry them, then iron the fabric pieces flat. Glue or sew ½" hems on opposite sides of the purple fabric. Make sure you have paper or fabric letters to spell "ONE SAVIOR—ONE KINGDOM."

GET SET...

Gather children and ask:

▶ **Why do people pledge their allegiance or loyalty to their country?**

Say: **People pledge their loyalty to a country to show they'll stand behind it and are proud of it. Not everyone thinks it's good to pledge allegiance to a country or a king. But Christians know it's wonderful to pledge our love, loyalty, and allegiance to Jesus Christ! Let's read what the Bible says about our one Lord.** Read aloud 1 Corinthians 8:6 and Ephesians 4:4-6. Then ask:

▶ **Why do you think it's wise to be loyal to Jesus?**

▶ **How can staying loyal to Jesus help us?**

▶ **In what ways can we stay true to Jesus?**

Say: **Being true to Jesus means following, loving, and serving him forever. We can stay true to Jesus** by reading the Bible, helping others, praying, and keeping Jesus as the focus of our lives. Pledging our love and loyalty to Jesus is the smartest thing we can do!

We all know that nations have flags. But did you know there's also a Christian flag? The Christian flag is red, white, and blue—but instead of stars, the Christian flag has a cross. Just as our national flag is a symbol for our country, the Christian flag is a symbol for Jesus our Savior and his heavenly kingdom. Let's make a beautiful banner with the Christian flag to symbolize the importance of following the one true Savior—Jesus!

GET CRAFTIN'...

Form groups called the Letter-Setters, the Flag-Fashioners, and the Braid Brigade. Spread the banner on the floor and be sure the hem pockets are at the top and the bottom of the banner. Have the Letter-Setters sort and glue pre-cut letters to the banner as shown in the illustration. Instruct the Flag-Fashioners to glue the blue box on the white fabric as shown, then cut a cross shape from red felt and glue it in the center of the blue box. Have the Braid Brigade glue gold fringe trim around the edges of the purple fabric. When the trim and letters are in place, glue the completed flag in the center of the purple fabric. Add gold braid at the top corners of the banner. Slide the dowel rods in the hem pockets, then add a length of gold braid for the hanger.

Present your labor of love to hang in the children's church room or some other location in your church building. Encourage children to explain to passersby that we want our love and loyalty to always remain in Jesus.

Crafty Tips
▶ Have each child make two small Christian flag bookmarks from construction paper, one to keep and one to give away. Write 1 Corinthians 8:6 on the back of the paper flag.
▶ This is a great craft idea for the Fourth of July or during June for Flag Day.

Crafty Tips
▶ Tell children the symbolism of the colors in the Christian flag: white for Jesus' purity, red for his blood, and blue for his heavenly kingdom. The purple banner and gold trim stand for Jesus' royalty.

The Super-Scene

I will walk in your truth. Psalm 86:11

Bible Craft Concept
God's truth is the basis of our lives.

Crafty Components
You'll need a Bible, a light blue or green shower curtain liner, permanent markers, newspapers, tempera paints, paintbrushes, a picture book, a felt-tipped pen, sandpaper, and duct tape.

GET READY...

Enlarge the illustrations of the indoor and outdoor scenes above. Select a picture book that has good background scenes.

GET SET...

Gather children in a group and hold up illustrations from the picture book. Point out the backgrounds in the pictures and ask children to identify details in the scenes. Then ask:

▶ **How do backgrounds help the pictures in a book?**

▶ **What if pictures didn't have any background scenes?**

▶ **In what ways do God's Word and his truth set a solid background for our lives?**

Say: **Background scenes help define stories and give us details so we understand what's going on in the pictures. That's just how God's truth is. It provides details so we understand how to live the way God wants us to. God's truth sets the stage for our lives by helping us be honest, loving, wise, thankful, and teachable. Let's read more about God's truth from the Bible.** Ask a volunteer to read aloud Psalm 25:5; 86:11; and 119:30. Then ask:

▶ **What are some of God's truths?**

▶ **How can using God's truth as a background for our lives help us every day?**

Say: **God's Word and his truth set an important background that helps us make wise decisions and allows us to trust God more. Every picture, skit, play, and movie needs a good background. But the most important background for our lives is God's truth. Let's make a nifty background scene to use in skits and Bible stories that will remind us of the importance of God's special background—his truth.**

GET CRAFTIN'...

Spread newspapers on the floor, then lay the shower curtain liner out flat. Show children the enlarged indoor and outdoor scenes you prepared, then let them choose which scene they'd like to make first. Use the felt-tipped pen to sketch the outline of the scene onto the shower curtain liner. Then invite children to use tempera paints and permanent markers to color the scene in vivid colors and patterns. Encourage children to try using lots of dots or tiny hearts to color an area instead of solid coloring. For a bumpy road, you may want to slide rough sandpaper under the shower curtain, then color over it. Paint is best for very large areas such as grass or sky. If your shower curtain liner is blue, don't bother painting the sky. If your liner is green, skip the grass.

When the curtain is dry, sketch and color the other side to make another scene. As children work, point out how handy this background will be for the whole church to use in skits, dramas, and plays, as well as for colorful room decorations. When both scenes are complete, let children put on a skit or retell a Bible story using the background scene. Simply use duct tape to attach the background to a wall or doorway. Donate your craft to your children's ministe to use in any number of ways.

Crafty Tips
▶ These scenes make wonderful beanbag toss targets for church carnivals!

Crafty Tips
▶ Use the background scenes as backdrops for classroom photos.

Crafty Tips
▶ Add bits of sandpaper, sponge, foil, cork, or wood-grained self-adhesive paper for real sensory-scene delight!

Giant Good-Fruit Grapevine

I am the vine; you are the branches. John 15:5

Bible Craft Concept
When we love Jesus, we do good things.

Crafty Components
You'll need a Bible, thick green florist's wire, green and purple construction paper, green metallic chenille wires, pencils, clear tape, purple raffia, scissors, and a bag of seedless red grapes.

GET READY...

Cut two 6' sections of green florist's wire. Be sure you have at least several yards of purple raffia. Raffia (dried grass) is available at most craft stores.

GET SET...

Gather children in a circle. Have them hold out their hands and close their eyes. Say: **I'm going to put something in your hands, but don't peek. Keep your eyes closed while we play a game about the object you're holding.** Hand each child a seedless red grape, then say: **Hold up your object if you think it's good to eat.** Pause. **Hold up your object if you think it's mentioned in the Bible.** Pause. **Now hold up your item if you think it's a lot like YOU!** Pause, then say: **I can see some of you are a little confused. Open your eyes and look at the object in your hands. You're all holding grapes—yummy fruit. Yes, grapes are mentioned in the Bible, and they're good to eat. But did you know the Bible wants us to be like good fruit, too? That's right!** Ask:

▶ **What is good fruit good for?**

▶ **Is bad fruit as useful as good fruit? Why or why not?**

▶ **In what ways are we like good fruit when we love Jesus?**

Say: **It may seem funny to compare us to good fruit, but that's what Jesus did. Let's read what Jesus said about who he is, who we are, and why we're to be like good fruit.** Read aloud John 15:5, 8. Then say: **Jesus said he is the vine and we are the branches that produce good fruit. When we're a part of Jesus, we love and follow him. We produce good fruit—that is, we can do good things with Jesus' help. What are some of the good things we can do when we love Jesus?** Encourage children to name things such as helping others, praying, and telling others about Jesus.

Say: **Jesus is the vine, and we are the branches that produce good fruit. That makes sense after all, doesn't it? Let's make huge vines with lots of good fruit to remind people that Jesus is the vine and we're the branches that bear good fruit.**

GET CRAFTIN'...

Form three groups: the Vine-Winders, the Leaf-Tearers, and the Grape-Bearers. Have the Vine-Winders curl green chenille wires around pencils to make vine curly-Q's, then wire the curly-Q's to the long pieces of florist's wire. Instruct the Leaf-Tearers to tear small green construction paper leaves and tape them down the length of the florist's wires. Leave about 4" of space between the leaves. The Grape-Bearers can cut out purple paper grapes and tape them into grape clusters to hang from the vines.

When the vines are finished, brainstorm types of "good fruit" we produce, such as helping others or telling others about Jesus. Write these ways on the clusters of grapes. Tape raffia bows to the ends of the vines, then hang the vines over doorways in the church, around pictures in the minister's office, or in the church entryway.

Crafty Tips
▶ For "compact" reminders of John 15:5, wind these lovely grapevines around grapevine wreaths from a craft store. Hang the wreaths on the front doors to the church.

Crafty Tips
▶ If you prefer, use small purple balloons for grape clusters.

Deck the Halls!

Enter his gates with thanksgiving and his courts with praise. Psalm 100:4

Bible Craft Concept
We take care of our church building.

Crafty Components
You'll need a Bible, tacky craft glue, colorful felt, scissors, gold fringe trim, and a 3'-by-6' length of white felt, satin, or velveteen.

GET READY...

If you're using satin or velveteen, be sure the fabric is "fray-proofed." Either hem the edges, use fusible webbing to press them under, or trim the edges with pinking shears.

GET SET...

Gather children and ask:

▶ **What things do you do to take care of your home? school? room? yard?**

▶ **How does keeping your room looking nice show you care about your home?**

▶ **How does caring for our church building show we care about God?**

Say: **When we take time to care for our church building, we're telling God we love him. Keeping our church looking special and clean is a way to show God we respect him and respect the special place he has given us to worship. Did you know there's a story in the Bible about a time another place of worship didn't look very nice? Let's read about that time and what happened when God's people cleaned the temple.**

Read aloud from 2 Kings 22:1-8 (or a Bible storybook) the story of the temple being repaired and the Book of the Law being found during the reign of Josiah. Then ask:

▶ **Why do you think Josiah wanted to clean and repair the temple?**

▶ **How can we take care of our own church building?**

Say: **God has given us the church as a special place to worship, learn about God, and help one another. It's important to take care of our church building and thank God for giving us this special place. Let's make a beautiful hallway hanging to decorate our church building with love and respect.**

GET CRAFTIN'...

Have children work in small groups to cut out felt heart, cross, and flower shapes they'd like to include. Encourage children to think about how their color choices might symbolize different truths, such as purple for Jesus' royalty, red for the blood Jesus shed on the cross, green for the everlasting life we have in Jesus, white for Christ's purity, and yellow for the warmth we have in Jesus' love and forgiveness. Have children limit their shape selection to hearts, crosses, and flowers—these are simple shapes to cut, and they will lend cohesion to the craft. Overlapping shapes, varying sizes, and effective use of color will create a pleasing effect!

When the shapes are cut, have children lay them on the white fabric and "play around" with the design until it's just as they want it. Then carefully glue the pieces in place. Finally, glue gold fringe on the short ends of the fabric and let children admire the beautiful results of their cooperative effort.

Have children wrap their lovely gift in tissue paper, then present it to the congregation at a predetermined time. Have your children explain the importance of keeping the church building in good repair and of beautifying the building as an act of love. Explain that this gift can be used as a wall hanging, a special "rug," or a table runner. End by leading the congregation in a prayer thanking God for your church building and for being a part of his loving church family.

Crafty Tips
▶ Younger children enjoy making lovely table runners for church potlucks by decorating 1'-by-2' lengths of cotton fabric with permanent markers.

Crafty Tips
▶ Check your local craft store for pre-cut fabric shapes. These "simply slick" iron-ons can be glued to fabric runners, then used as great "community" gifts for nursing homes, homeless shelters, and children's homes.

Funtabulous Felt Storyboard

They never stopped teaching and proclaiming the good news that Jesus is the Christ. Acts 5:42

Bible Craft Concept
We like to teach others about Jesus.

Crafty Components
You'll need a Bible, tacky craft glue, markers, scissors, bright ribbon, a stapler, poster board, felt, a large envelope, a Bible story coloring book, a 2 ½-by-4 ½' piece of dark blue or black felt, and a 2'-by-4' acoustic ceiling panel.

GET READY...

Ask the workers at a construction site for an acoustic ceiling panel or purchase one from any builders supply store.

GET SET...

Gather children and ask:

▶ **What's a favorite story you've heard?**

▶ **Why is it fun to tell and hear special stories?**

▶ **In what ways can we learn from hearing stories?**

Say: **The Bible is filled with wonderful stories. And the best thing about Bible stories is—they're real! When we read Bible stories about Jesus, we learn about who Jesus was and why he came into the world. We learn that Jesus was God's Son who was sent to love us. We also learn how Jesus wants us to live and treat others.**

▶ **What would it be like if we never heard Bible stories?**

▶ **What are some of your favorite "Jesus stories"?**

Have children take turns reading aloud the story of Jesus calming the storm from Matthew 8:23-27. Then ask:

▶ **What did this Bible story teach you about Jesus? about trusting Jesus? about not being afraid?**

▶ **Why is it important to teach people about Jesus?**

▶ **How can we teach others about Jesus?**

Say: **In the Bible, we learn of some people who never stopped teaching about Jesus.** Read aloud Acts 5:42. **We can teach others about Jesus, too, by telling them Bible stories. And we can tell the stories in a fun way—with the special Bible storyboard we'll make!**

GET CRAFTIN'...

Form two groups, the Construction Board and the Picture-Producers. Have the Construction Board cover the acoustic ceiling panel with the large piece of felt. Carefully staple the felt behind the panel, pulling the fabric to remove wrinkles. When the fabric is securely stapled in place, glue ribbon to the edge of the covered side to make a colorful "frame." Flip the storyboard over and staple a large envelope to the back to hold story pictures.

While the Construction Board is working, have the Picture-Producers choose, color, and cut out story pictures from the Bible story coloring book. Favorite stories might include Jesus' birth, Jesus calming the sea, Jesus feeding the five thousand, or the Easter story. Glue the pictures to poster board for stability, then cut out the poster board pictures. Glue small swatches of felt to the backs of the pictures so they'll "stick" to the felt storyboard. Prepare enough pictures for at least three stories.

When the Bible storyboard and story pictures are finished, invite children to take turns telling the Bible stories and using the story pictures to make up question-and-answer games. Then invite another class to listen to your special "story hour." Store the story pictures in the envelope on the back of the storyboard. Donate the storyboard to a younger children's class, your children's minister, or a children's hospital.

Crafty Tips

▶ For a creative twist, let children fashion story characters out of colorful construction paper. Glue the figures to poster board, then add small felt squares to the backs of the figures.

Crafty Tips

▶ Make small storyboards by gluing felt to plastic clipboards. Create story pictures from construction paper, then keep them in an envelope clipped to the felt board for "instant story times."

Joyous Window-Wow! - - - -

I have told you this so that my joy may be in you and that your joy may be complete. John 15:11

Bible Craft Concept
There's joy in loving Jesus!

Crafty Components
You'll need a Bible, water-based markers, newsprint, clear tape, pencils, clear packing tape, a can of hair spray, and a 1' square of clear plastic vinyl for each child.

GET READY...

You can purchase clear plastic vinyl by the yard from most fabric stores. This thin vinyl will cling to glass like "static stick-ons."

GET SET...

Have children form trios and tell their trio members two things that bring them joy. When you clap your hands, have each trio join another trio and tell the new group members what brings each person joy. Continue clapping and joining trios until the children are in one large group. Then ask:

▶ **What is joy?**

▶ **How is joy different from simply being happy?**

▶ **Where can we find real joy?**

Say: **Joy is a very special happiness. It doesn't come from sunshine, and it can't be bought with money. Real joy isn't something you earn or find sitting on a store shelf. Real joy comes from just one place. Do you know who gives us real joy?** Let children tell their ideas. Then say: **I'll read something from the Bible. When you know where real joy comes from, jump up and clap two times.** Read aloud John 15:9-11, then jump up and clap two times. Say: **Who gives us real joy? Jesus! Jesus is the only place where true** joy comes from. When we have the joy of Jesus, we can love and help other people and share that joy all around the world. Nothing stops the joy of Jesus! And each time we see the beautiful colors in stained glass windows, we're reminded of the joy we have in Jesus. So let's make pretend stained glass windows to share that joy with others.

GET CRAFTIN'...

Have children re-form their original trios. Explain that each person will make a part of a huge stained glass display. Hand each child a sheet of newsprint and a pencil. Instruct children to sketch a simple design with large spaces to color. For example, kids might sketch a dove, a heart, a Bible story picture, or words such as joy, Jesus, or peace. Then tape each piece of newsprint behind a square of vinyl and let children use markers to color in the designs that show through. Encourage children to use bright colors. When the designs are complete, remove the newsprint and spray the squares of vinyl with hair spray to "seal" the marker against smears and smudges. Then tape the squares together with clear packing tape to make one or more large "stained glass windows."

Have children choose a large window in which to display their labor of love. The plastic should cling to the window without tape. Windows that face the street are a fine choice! Or donate your joy-filled design to be placed in a sanctuary window for the entire congregation to en-JOY!

Crafty Tips
▶ Use simple drawings from Bible story coloring books for "traceable" designs and pictures.

Crafty Tips
▶ Tape the vinyl squares in the shape of a cross for an interesting effect.

Super Sensational Ceiling

By understanding he set the heavens in place. Proverbs 3:19

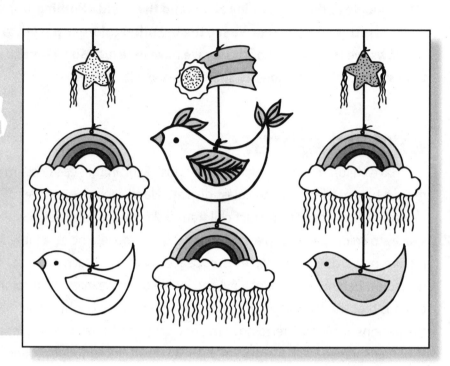

Bible Craft Concept
God made the heavens for us to enjoy.

Crafty Components
You'll need a Bible, markers, paper plates, scissors, fishing line, bingo daubers, tape, glue, poster board, glitter glue, cotton balls, craft feathers, colored tissue paper, and tinsel or shredded foil.

GET READY...

Photocopy the patterns on page 96 onto stiff paper. Then set up three craft centers. Place the star and comet patterns, markers, tinsel, and glitter glue at the Perfect Planet center. Place paper plates, glue, cotton balls, tinsel or foil, and bingo daubers at the Rad Rainbows center. Place the bird patterns, craft feathers, glue, and markers at the Feathery Friends center. Put scissors at each craft center.

GET SET...

Gather children in a circle and have them close their eyes. Say: **Let's pretend we're outside on a beautiful sunny day. Look up into the sky—what do you see that God made?** Encourage children to use their imaginations to tell what they "see." Special sights might include birds, the sun, clouds, rain, and rainbows. **Now let's make believe it's nighttime. Look at the sky—what do you see that God made?** Night-sights might include stars, comets, planets, and the moon. Have children open their eyes, then ask:

▶ **Why do you suppose God made so many wonderful things in the heavens?**

▶ **What might it be like if God hadn't made all those things for us?**

▶ **What are your favorite "heavenly" sights?**

Say: **The Bible tells us that God made the heavens through his wisdom and love. Let's read about the**

heavenly wonders God made. Read aloud Genesis 1:1-8, 14-19; Proverbs 3:19; and Psalm 8:3-5. Then say: **God made each part of the heavens for us to enjoy. The sun helps us see clearly in daytime and makes foods grow. The clouds bring rain that gives us water to drink. And we know that God made the rainbow as a symbol of his promise never to flood the world again. God made the moon to give us light at night, and he made the stars to twinkle a while and make us smile! Wow! Just think of all that God made!** Ask:

▶ **How do the heavens show God's love for us?**

Say: **Each time we look into the sky—whether it's day or night—we're reminded of God's powerful love for us. We can't make heavenly objects like God did, but we can have fun making pretend ones to remind us that God made the heavens for us to enjoy.**

GET CRAFTIN'...

Have children form trios. Explain that each trio will be making three heavenly objects: a Perfect Planet, a Rad Rainbow, and a Feathery Friend. Have each trio decide which member will make each item and then go to the appropriate craft center. To make Perfect Planets, choose a pattern, trace and color it, then cut the object out. Embellish stars and comets with tinsel "tails" and glitter glue. To make each Rad Rainbow, cut paper plates in half and glue tinsel or foil across the straight bottom of the plate half. Glue cotton ball "clouds" to the center of the plate and color rainbow stripes above the clouds. To fashion a Feathery Friend, trace, color, and cut out a bird pattern. Then glue colorful craft feathers on the fun-fowl.

When each trio member has finished his or her contribution, connect each trio's objects by taping them to a 4' length of fishing line. Suspend your heavenly mobiles from the ceiling of a drab hallway with the following sign:

Look around at all God's made—
His wondrous creation on parade!
God made the world with love divine—
Thank you, God, for your loving design!

If you'd like, make copies of the "thank you rhyme." Then hand them out to church members, along with individual stars, birds, or rainbows. What a heavenly lift you'll bring to others!

Crafty Tips
▶ These glittery, glitzy stars and planets make great bulletin board craft ideas!

Crafty Tips
▶ If your class is very large, make another craft center and add a yellow cellophane sun and silver glitter moon to the mobiles.

Photocopy these patterns.

Chapter 5

MAMMOTH MUNCHIES

Delectable bread baked in flower-pots, super-sized subs, and a feast of other tasty treats!

Fiery Furnace Fudgies

Do not worship any other god. Exodus 34:14

Bible Craft Concept
We worship God even when the "heat is on"!

Crafty Components
You'll need a Bible, a roll of aluminum foil, tape, plastic spoons, and two packages each of chocolate chips, mini-marshmallows, and graham crackers.

GET READY...

This outdoor activity needs a sunny summer day—and lots of hungry kids!

GET SET...

Gather the children and ask:

▶ **What is "worship"?**

▶ **Who are we to worship and why?**

Say: **Worship is a way to show God that we love him, respect him, recognize his power, and want to know him more. We worship God because God is worthy of praise. We worship God to grow closer to him. In other words, we worship God because we love him! Just imagine how awful it would be if someone told us we couldn't worship God! But that's what happened to three friends in the Bible. A wicked king told the friends to stop loving and worshiping God, but they wouldn't. Let's read this exciting story. When you hear how God helped the friends, put your hands on your hearts.** Retell or read aloud the story of Shadrach, Meshach, and Abednego from a Bible storybook. Then ask:

▶ **Why did God send angels to help the friends?**

▶ **What did you learn about worshiping God no matter what?**

Say: **God wants us to never stop worshiping him. To stop worshiping God, we'd have to stop loving God—and that wouldn't happen in a million years, no siree! Let's make a pretend fiery furnace and cook up a delicious snack to share with others. Then we can tell them how important it is to worship God no matter what!**

GET CRAFTIN'...

Tape five 5' lengths of aluminum foil side by side to make a huge square "cookie sheet." Be sure children have clean hands, then have them lay all the graham crackers on one half of the foil. Next, have children sprinkle both packages of chocolate chips over the graham crackers. Finally, sprinkle both bags of mini-marshmallows over the chocolate chips. Loosely fold the opposite half of the foil over the graham cracker mixture, then pinch the foil edges together to keep the wind from blowing the foil open.

Invite another class or two to enjoy listening to the story of Shadrach, Meshach, and Abednego as the "fiery furnace" treats melt in the sunshine. Encourage your children to point out the importance of worshiping God even if someone criticizes us or tells us we shouldn't. After ten minutes, carefully unwrap the fudgie treats and hand each person a plastic spoon. Then enjoy the treats right from the foil! As children eat, visit about the three friends from the Bible story and how God protected them by sending angels. Point out how God was pleased that Shadrach, Meshach, and Abednego worshiped him, so God protected them in the furnace.

When you're finished eating, toss the foil in the trash for cleanup in a snap!

Crafty Tips
▶ If the day isn't sunny or hot, substitute marshmallow creme for the mini-marshmallows. Simply drizzle the marshmallow creme over the treats!

Crafty Tips
▶ Copy the recipe for fiery furnace fudgies onto an index card, then run off copies for children to take home.

Super Servant "Sundae"

Anything you did for any of my people here, you also did for me. Matthew 25:40

Bible Craft Concept
When we serve others, we serve Jesus.

Crafty Components
You'll need a Bible, cake donuts from a bakery, paper plates, plastic spoons, containers of whipped cream, serving spoons, and several containers of strawberry topping or frozen strawberries.

GET READY...

Purchase enough cake donuts so you'll have a donut for each person you're planning on serving. Decide whether to serve another class or the entire congregation.

GET SET...

This edible service craft idea is perfect for any Sunday evening get-together or church picnic. Gather children and ask:

▶ **When's a time someone served you?**

▶ **Did you enjoy being served? Why or why not?**

▶ **What are ways to serve others?**

▶ **How does serving someone show our love for that person? for Jesus?**

Say: **Many people think only kings and queens are special enough to be served. But Jesus spent his life serving everyone he met, rich and poor alike. In fact, Jesus taught us that to be truly great in God's kingdom, we must become servants of everyone we meet. Jesus also said that when we serve other people, we're really serving him, too. What do you think Jesus meant by this?** Allow children to tell their ideas. Then say: **Let's see what the Bible says about serving others.** Read aloud Matthew 25:34-40. Then say:

Jesus served others by helping them, feeding them, teaching them about God's love, and praying for them. Ask:

▶ **How did Jesus' servanthood demonstrate his love?**

▶ **How can we serve others to show our love?**

Say: **Let's serve up a bit of tasty fun! We'll make a super strawberry sundae to practice serving others and to remind everyone that when we serve others, we're also serving Jesus.**

Crafty Tips
▶ If you prefer, use small vanilla wafer cookies instead of donuts.

GET CRAFTIN'...

Let children cover a table top with paper plates. Then have kids form three groups: the Donut Dealers, the Strawberry Toppings, and the Whipped Cream Team. Explain to the children that they'll prepare this edible craft in an "assembly line." First, the Donut Dealers can place a plain cake donut on each plate. Then the Strawberry Toppings can spoon strawberries over each donut. Finally, the Whipped Cream Team will place a dollop of whipped cream on top of each "Servant Sundae."

When the Super Servant Sundaes are ready, invite the guests you planned to serve. Hand guests plastic spoons and help them find comfortable places to sit. Then have your class serve each guest a strawberry sundae "with a smile." Before you enjoy the special treats, invite your children to say a prayer thanking the guests for attending and asking God's help in serving one another with love.

While people nibble their sundaes, have your children read aloud Matthew 25:34-40 and explain that these special sundaes are one way they'd like to serve their friends and tell them how special they are. You may wish to have several volunteers from your class read aloud the story of Jesus serving his disciples by washing their feet at the last supper (John 13:1-17). End the activity by serving as the cleanup crew and making sure the eating area is spic and span!

Crafty Tips
▶ For a "surprise service," have your children carefully carry the Servant Sundaes to the room with the people you plan to serve. Shhh—don't tell them you're coming! What a yummy surprise!

Wise Men Spice Tea

We...have come to worship him. Matthew 2:2

Bible Craft Concept
We can honor Jesus with our gifts and talents.

Crafty Components
You'll need a Bible, a new wastebasket, several jars of instant tea and instant orange breakfast drink, cinnamon, a paper punch, spoons, and two dozen baby food jars with lids. You'll also need tacky craft glue, ribbon, cinnamon sticks, and copies of the direction card on page 103.

GET READY...

Photocopy as many direction cards as there are jars. Cut out the cards. Purchase small cinnamon sticks at most craft stores. If you can't find cinnamon sticks, use cloves instead.

GET SET...

Gather children in a circle. Ask children to share with the group any special talents, hobbies, or interests they may have. Then ask:

▶ **How can people use their special talents and gifts to honor Jesus?**

▶ **Why is it important for us to honor Jesus?**

Say: **We honor Jesus because we love him and want him to know how special he is in our lives. But do you know what the great part about honoring Jesus is? Everyone has his or her own ways to honor Jesus! Some people have special talents they can honor Jesus with, such as repairing the church or painting lovely pictures to cheer others. Some people honor Jesus by singing special songs about his love. And others honor Jesus by teaching Sunday school or helping someone who is sick. When Jesus was born, some wise men wanted to visit Jesus to honor him through worship and giving. Let's read how the wise men honored Jesus.** Read aloud Matthew 2:1-11, then ask:

▶ **What gifts did the wise men bring to honor Jesus?**

▶ **How did worshiping and giving gifts to Jesus honor him?**

▶ **How can you honor Jesus this week?**

Say: **The story of the wise men helps us understand how important it is to honor Jesus in our own ways. The wise men honored Jesus through worship and giving. We can honor Jesus by making special gifts that will remind others how important it is to honor Jesus.**

Crafty Tips
▶ Use any recipe for instant cocoa mix and fill jars with hot cocoa mix instead of tea.

GET CRAFTIN'...

Place the new wastebasket in the center of the room. Form two groups, the Tea-Makers and the Jar-tists. Have the Tea-Makers pour the cinnamon and the jars of tea and instant orange drink mix into the new wastebasket. Mix the dry ingredients thoroughly. While the tea is being mixed, have the Jar-tists glue cinnamon sticks to the tops of the baby food jars. When the tea is thoroughly mixed, spoon the spice tea into jars until each jar is filled. Tightly replace the jar lids.

Have children punch holes in the photocopied cards, then thread ribbon through the holes and tie the cards to the necks of the tea jars. Place the jars of tea in a large box, then brainstorm where your class would like to donate their special offering. Consider nursing homes, older church members, or senior centers. What an especially nice way to honor Jesus while giving to others at Christmas!

Crafty Tips
▶ Have children make holiday gifts for church leaders. Prepare jars of spice tea, then decorate ceramic mugs with acrylic paints.

Wise Men Spice Tea

Directions: Use two teaspoons of instant spice tea mix per cup of hot water. Stir well, enjoy, and remember...
"We have come to worship him." Matthew 2:2

Share-With-Others Sculpture

Share with God's people who are in need. Romans 12:13

Bible Craft Concept
We can share with those in need.

Crafty Components
You'll need a Bible, a plastic laundry basket, crepe paper, clear tape, balloons, twine, duct tape, paper cups and plates, markers, plastic flatware, and a variety of packaged foods.

GET READY...

Purchase packaged foods such as canned fruits and vegetables, jars of peanut butter and jelly, bread, chips, cake mix, canned icing, boxes of macaroni and cheese, and canned tuna. This service craft idea should cost around $15, but it is a wonderful way for your church to provide for a community outreach!

GET SET...

Gather children in a group. Ask:

▶ **How do you feel when you're hungry?**

▶ **What's your favorite meal?**

▶ **What would it be like if you never had your favorite meal again? if you didn't have much food at all?**

Say: **We all eat very well—fruits, vegetables, meats, and potatoes. Not many of us go to bed hungry at night. But there are people who are less fortunate than we are. These people may not get enough to eat and probably never have their favorite foods—or even know what their favorite foods are! Think of how hard that would be! Jesus helped feed many hungry people. In fact, once Jesus fed five thousand people at one time! Let's read the story of how Jesus fed these people. When you hear what foods Jesus provided, pat your tummies.** Read aloud Matthew 14:13-21 and Romans 12:13. Then ask:

▶ **Why do you think Jesus fed the hungry people?**

▶ **How can we be like Jesus and help hungry people?**

Say: **We can help a family less fortunate than we are by making them a neat food sculpture to enjoy!**

GET CRAFTIN'...

Form two groups—one to prepare the party basket and one to make the food sculpture. To prepare the basket, have children weave colorful crepe paper streamers in and out of the openings in the basket. Tape "bouquets" of uninflated balloons around the sides of the basket for a festive touch. Have children cut several crepe paper streamers and write joyful messages or Scripture verses on them, then tape the streamers to the top edges of the basket.

Have the children making the food sculpture use their imaginations, twine, and duct tape to attach the containers of food together. Point out that boxes, cans, and jars of equal height stack together well and add stability to the sculpture. Show children how to roll pieces of duct tape and tape plastic flatware, paper cups, and plates to the edible artwork.

When the basket and food sculpture are complete, carefully place the sculpture in the basket. Then donate your wonderful edible sculpture to a less fortunate family, older couple, or women's shelter.

Crafty Tips

▶ When shopping for food items, try to select equal-sized cans and jars for easier stacking.

Crafty Tips

▶ Use this festive idea for a Christmas dinner delight! Use a mammoth decorated box with bows and tinsel instead of a laundry basket. Be sure to wrap and include a few inexpensive surprise gifts such as small toys and games, pretty soaps, and cute toothbrushes.

Really Big Root Beer Float

For he has delivered me from all my troubles. Psalm 54:7

Bible Craft Concept
When we're worried, Jesus keeps us "afloat."

Crafty Components
You'll need a Bible, a large new plastic wastebasket, markers, plastic cups, drinking straws, clear packing tape, ladles, and ice cream scoops. You'll also need three to five bottles of root beer and two or three half-gallon containers of vanilla ice cream for every twenty-five children.

GET READY...

For inexpensive root beer and ice cream, purchase generic labels or ask volunteer parents to donate the goodies for your class outreach. This is a great icebreaker or kickoff for VBS or any children's summer program!

GET SET...

Gather children and ask:

▶ **What helps save your life if you're drowning?**

▶ **How does a lifesaver or life preserver work?**

▶ **In what ways is Jesus like a lifesaver?**

Say: **A lifesaver keeps us afloat when we're drowning. Troubles and worries are a lot like a deep lake. Worries can wash over us and make us feel as though we're drowning—we don't know how to save ourselves. But when we give our worries to Jesus, he is like our special lifesaver who helps us stay afloat! Let's read what the Bible says about Jesus helping us.** Read aloud Hebrews 13:6, Psalm 54:7, and 2 Timothy 1:8-10. Then ask:

▶ **How can giving our worries to Jesus help?**

▶ **Can we save ourselves? Why or why not?**

Have children each silently think of one worry they can give to Jesus, then say: **Let's pray for Jesus to help us stay afloat with our worries. I'll pray, and when I pause, you can silently name one worry you'll give to Jesus. Ready? Dear Lord, we thank you for all the help you give us when we're afraid, lonely, or worried. We're so glad that Jesus loves us enough to help us stay afloat! Right now, I'm giving this worry to Jesus.** Pause. **Thank you, Lord, for your love. Amen.**

Now let's make a special treat to remind us that when we give our worries to Jesus, he helps us stay afloat. We'll invite another class to share our gigantic root beer float and learn how important it is to give their worries to Jesus, too.

GET CRAFTIN'...

This edible service craft idea is best suited for outdoors. Place the large new plastic wastebasket outside on cement or level ground. Have children invite another class to join them, then hand each person four drinking straws and a plastic cup. Set out the markers and invite children to decorate their cups in a festive fashion. Then show children how to connect their straws by pinching one end of each straw and pushing it into the end of another straw. Tape around the "straw connection." Continue adding straws until each child has a "four-story straw."

Let children cooperatively pour root beer into the container and add scoops of ice cream until the root beer and ice cream are gone. Ladle root beer and ice cream into the plastic cups—or enjoy your gigantic root beer float right from the huge "root beer mug." As you sip your cool treats, point out how the ice cream floats. Then have your children tell the other class that Jesus is the one who keeps us afloat when we have worries or troubles.

Crafty Tips
▶ Reusable plastic mugs work great for this activity—and they can be used all year long if children write their names on them!

Crafty Tips
▶ Instead of root beer, try using fruit-flavored soft drink mix.

Humongous Heroes

Who is this King of glory? The Lord strong and mighty. Psalm 24:8

Bible Craft Concept
Jesus is our one true hero.

Crafty Components
You'll need a Bible, white paper, a marker, a sharp knife, waxed paper, plastic knives, three loaves of French bread, lettuce, ham, cheese, baloney, pickle slices, napkins, and the following condiments: mustard, mayonnaise, and ketchup.

GET READY...

Cover a table with waxed paper, then set out the ingredients. This recipe will make about twelve snack sandwiches. Keep a sharp knife nearby but out of reach of children.

GET SET...

Have children form pairs or trios. Write the word "HEROES" on the white paper and hold it up. Challenge each pair or trio to brainstorm who the greatest heroes in the world are and why. Then have each group tell its answers. Ask:

▶ **What makes a hero great?**

Say: **There are heroes in the world, such as people who save others from fires or drowning. These people do amazing things to help others even when their own lives are in danger. But many people seem to think that heroes are those who play sports or race cars or play wild music.** Ask:

▶ **Are these people true heroes? Why or why not?**

▶ **Is Jesus a true hero? Explain.**

▶ **Are false "heroes" worthy of our praise? Explain.**

▶ **Is Jesus worthy of our praise as a true hero? Why?**

Say: **Jesus is our one true hero. We don't want to be misled by false heroes, and we don't want to worship them. Jesus is the one true hero worthy of our praise and thanks.** Read aloud Psalm 24:7-10. Then say: **Jesus died to save our lives and the lives of everyone who loves him. And Jesus rose again to show us that we'll live forever with him in heaven! You can think of it like this: There are many false heroes, but HE-ROSE to save us!** Write the words "HE-ROSE" on the white paper. **Pretty neat, isn't it? We can worship the one true hero in all the world! Let's celebrate how glad we are that Jesus is our hero by making a huge hero sandwich to share with others. Then we'll invite people to celebrate with us!**

GET CRAFTIN'...

Cut the loaves of French bread in half lengthwise, then cut one loaf in half again widthwise. Help children place the bottoms of the two long loaves end to end on the waxed paper. Place the two short bottom halves on either side to make a "cross." Have children cooperatively place lettuce, ham, cheese, baloney, and pickle slices on the bread, then replace the bread "tops." As you work, decide who you'd like to invite to your "hero celebration." Visit about the miraculous things Jesus did for others, such as healing the sick, helping the lame to walk, calming the sea, and feeding the hungry. Point out again that there may be false heroes, but "he-rose" to be our one true hero!

Set napkins beside the giant hero sandwich, and be sure the plastic knives and condiments are nearby. When everyone is present, invite several of your children to explain that Jesus is our one true hero and why. Have children show your guests the paper with the words "HE-ROSE" and explain its significance. Share a prayer thanking Jesus for his love and salvation, then share a feast of hero snack sandwiches by cutting the larger sandwich into 3" pieces.

Crafty Tips

▶ For a larger group, use hamburger buns to make small hero sandwiches. Spell out the word "HEROSE," then explain the unusual spelling of the word to your guests.

Crafty Tips

▶ Make this super sub during the Easter season and enjoy a real feast as you read aloud the Easter story and visit about why Jesus is our one true hero.

Giant Garden of Life Bread

I am the bread of life. John 6:35

Front

Back

Bible Craft Concept
Jesus' love nurtures us.

Crafty Components
You'll need a Bible, non-stick cooking spray, several new 10" clay flowerpots, tacky craft glue, aluminum foil, mixing bowls and spoons, ribbon, markers or tempera paints, a knife, and ingredients for the recipe below.

GET READY...

Since this wonderful service craft idea needs baking, be sure you have access to an oven. This clever idea will take about an hour and a half—but it's well worth the extra time!

GET SET...

Gather children in a group and ask:

▶ **What does bread do for us?**

▶ **How can bread keep us alive?**

▶ **How is Jesus like bread that gives life?**

Say: **In the Bible, Jesus called himself the bread of life. Let's read what Jesus said.** Read aloud John 6:35. Then ask: **What do you think Jesus meant by this?** Encourage children to share their ideas, then say: **Jesus knew that people often eat bread to stay alive. He knew that people would understand how important bread can be to their survival. And Jesus also knew**

Garden of Life Bread

(Makes 1 flowerpot of bread)

Cream 1/2 cup shortening and 1 cup white sugar. Add 2 eggs and beat well. Stir in 1 mashed banana. Add 1 1/4 cup flour, 3/4 teaspoon baking soda, 1/2 teaspoon salt. Mix well. Pour into a greased 10" clay flowerpot. Bake at 375 degrees for 60 to 70 minutes or until bread is lightly browned.

how very important he is to our survival—both in this world and in heaven. **Jesus called himself the bread of life because his love gives us life on earth and his death brings us life in heaven. Jesus nourishes and nurtures us with his love so we grow closer to him and to God.**

We all know that grain to make bread grows in gardens and fields. Let's make wonderful pots of "Garden of Life Bread" to remind others that Jesus is the bread of life.

GET CRAFTIN'...

Explain that you'll be mixing bread, then baking it in clean garden pots. Have children form as many groups as you have clay pots. Help children mix the bread in bowls according to the bread recipe. Spray the insides of the pots with non-stick cooking spray. Cover the drainage hole in the bottom of each pot with a small piece of aluminum foil. Then spoon the lumpy batter into the pot. Bake immediately. While the bread is baking, read aloud John 6:32-40 and visit about the ways Jesus brings us life and "feeds" us with his love and forgiveness.

When the bread is baked and has cooled for about ten minutes, loosen the bread around the edges with a knife. Glue a ribbon around each pot and tie a fluffy bow. Have children use markers or tempera paints to write the words "Jesus Is the Bread of Life" on the sides of each pot. You may wish to cover the bread with clear plastic wrap. Then present your special gifts of love to a retirement home, a senior recreation center, or a food pantry.

Crafty Tips
▶ This project makes a great fund-raiser for children to collect money for missionaries or local charities.

Crafty Tips
▶ Instead of baking the bread, simply place packaged quick-bread mix inside pots and present them with baking instructions.

INDEX